BARBARO

B A R

A NATION'S LOVE STORY

Tom Philbin and Pamela K. Brodowsky

B A R O

An Imprint of HarperCollinsPublishers

HarperCollins books may be purchased for educational, business,
or sales promotional use. For information, please write:
Special Markets Department, HarperCollins Publishers,
10 East 53rd Street, New York, NY 10022.

FIRST EDITION

Designed by Sunil Manchikanti

Library of Congress Cataloging-in-Publication Data is available upon request.

ISBN: 978-0-06-128485-4
ISBN-10: 0-06-128485-8

07   08   09   10   11   DIX/RRD   10   9   8   7   6   5   4   3   2   1

Acknowledgments

We would like to thank the following people for their help in the making of *Barbaro*: Headley Bell, Chris Drolet, Dan Blacker, Dr. Lawrence Bramlage, Bill and Sandy Sanborn, and Bob Frieze. With a special thanks to Roy and Gretchen Jackson along with Michael Matz for providing us with this wonderful creature who made the writing of this book all the more interesting.

For Barbaro

April 29, 2003–January 29, 2007

PAM AND TOM

Contents

Introduction

This book is a biography about a great racehorse, how he came to be, how he was trained, how he made electricity ripple through over 150,000 people at Churchill Downs on May 6, 2006, as he burst from the pack at the top of stretch and we watched, mouths agape, as he pulled away from that pack with every stride and heard the announcer yelling, "It's all Barbaro! It's all Barbaro!"

And it's about this magnificent creature who captured the interest of racing fans like few other horses in racing history, because they knew he had a good chance to become the first Triple Crown winner in 28 years.

And it's about bringing realization to the dream of his owners, Gretchen and Roy Jackson, their dream to own a champion horse.

But it is also a story about love, a nation's love for a horse, about a beautiful creature who broke down in front of millions of people at Pimlico Racetrack who immediately held their breath and wondered if this great horse was going to die or, more specifically, be "put down."

It is also a story of courage and belief and tears, and a veterinarian surgeon, Dr. Dean Richardson, who was in Palm Beach, Florida, watching the Preakness Stakes on a television and saw this great horse "break down," holding his right hind leg up. That doctor knew immediately that it was a severe injury, and when he received the animal X rays, which are called radiographs, he knew that he was not going to be sleeping well that night. Tomorrow morning, when the sun came up, he would be on an airplane heading north to the hospital where this great horse would be waiting and that doctor would be picking up the scalpel trying to save this horse's life as the world watched. His task was daunting. He would have to put a leg together that had been shattered into something like twenty pieces. And he didn't know for sure if he could do it.

But this veterinarian knew that if anyone could, he could, and this was exactly why he had become a doctor. He was known in the medical community as a surgeon with a mind like a razor—he literally wrote the books on equine surgery—and with great hands, but beneath it all, a long time before he had become head of New Bolton Hospital, he had as a young man become acquainted with horses for the first time and had learned to love them. And it was that love that was in his heart, as that plane lifted off from Miami International Airport, that was the driving force behind the hands and the mind and everything else.

It is also a story about the love of Barbaro's owners, people who had a clear choice: let the horse be euthanized, collect an obscene amount of insurance money, and let time heal. Or fight for the horse's life.

This is a story about a great trainer and a great jockey and about ordinary people from all over America who unleashed a torrent of love that lifted the spirits of everyone involved with this terribly hurt and threatened horse. This love helped give them the strength and courage to see this crisis through to the end. After all, if a little girl could send Barbaro a bottle of aspirin—and one did—because it helped her mother deal with pain and "maybe" could help him also, what were we adults to do?

Everything we could.

Ultimately, maybe, it's a story about us. People who could love and care about an innocent creature so, so much. We, who could not, would not let this horse die.

BARBARO

Once there was a little girl who loved a horse named Whirlaway . . .
—**Tom Philbin and Pamela K. Brodowsky**

Quest for a Champion

*I*n 1941, there existed a crazy thorough-bred horse named "Whirlaway," a small chestnut colt who stood fifteen "hands" high (each hand is 4" wide). His trainer, the great Ben A. Jones, characterized him as being as nervous as "a cat in a room full of rocking chairs" and not too bright. "You could teach him," Jones said, "but you couldn't teach him much."

Whirlaway, the great Eddie Arcaro up, and trainer Ben Jones. When Barbaro's other mom, Gretchen Jackson, was a little girl, she loved this horse, who was crazy, slow-witted, and superfast all at the same time.

In fact, one might say, just looking at his tail made him seem crazy. Instead of being like most horses', which were trimmed at the hocks, he had a tail that went almost all the way to the ground. Indeed, his nickname was "Mr. Longtail." But it was kept long for a reason. When he was running, the tail would stretch out and flail at other horses, who would automatically keep their distance from this nervous horse.

Jones tolerated Whirlaway for one simple reason: As someone once said, "He could outrun the wind."

Indeed, he could. In the Kentucky Derby, he ran the fastest time ever, 2:01 and ⅖, a time that would stand until 1962, and he also became that rarest of creatures—winner of the Triple Crown, also winning both the Preakness and Belmont Stakes.

At the time, Whirlaway had many admirers, not only because he was fast but because of his eccentricities—you never knew what he was going to do when he ran—known all over the country, indeed the world. And one of those who knew was a little girl who lived in Pennsylvania named Gretchen, who, like others, had a black-and-white picture of him. She would spend much time looking at the horse—studying him.

Gretchen, as it happened, loved horses, and unlike some things in childhood that prove to be flashes in the pan, her love for horses endured. And one day in 2006, Gretchen Jackson would be watching as a horse she had dreamed about for 30 years—her Whirlaway—who was named Barbaro, a small Peruvian man on his back, was bursting out of a pack of horses as they entered the stretch and drove to the wire to win in the ultimate horse race, the Kentucky Derby, by 6½ lengths, the biggest margin of victory in over 60 years.

As Gretchen watched, standing next to her was another horse lover, her husband, Roy, who had dreamed along with her.

The Jacksons could hardly have predicted that Barbaro would turn out to be, as it were, Barbaro. They own Lael (it means loyalty) Farms in West Grove, Pennsylvania, and had been breeding horses for many years. But they had never succeeded in developing one that was winning any big races in the United States, though they did have a winner of a big race in England. They nursed a dream of winning big for 30 years.

Still, there was no guarantee that you would breed a champion no matter what you did. The main thing was a horse's pedigree, but that was no guarantee of performance either. A foal's mother could be the 1980 Derby winner, "Genuine Risk," and its father "Man o' War," perhaps the greatest racehorse who ever lived, one's grandfather "Secretariat"—who was the first horse to cover the 1¼-mile Derby track in under two minutes, and one's grandmother the 1915 Derby winner, "Regret," and nothing was guaranteed. Far from it.

Indeed, some of the colts who produced champions could make one blink with disbelief. One such was "Reigh Count," a colt owned by John D. Hertz, a wily ex-boxer who owned the Yellow Cab Company and who would go on to start Hertz Rent A Car. Reigh Count won the 1928 Kentucky Derby as well as other significant stakes races, including the Saratoga Cup, the Huron Handicap, the Jockey Club Gold Cup, and, in England, the Ascot Gold Cup. After he retired to stud, Reigh Count was a successful sire for the Hertzes, but none of his offspring was a Derby winner. Then Hertz, ever the innovator, had a crazy idea: Instead of breeding or mating Reigh Count to famous, high-priced mares, he bred him—mystifyingly—to a tired old horse named, ironically, "Quickly."

The "covering"—the trade term for the sex act between horses—was successful, but when the foal was born, people were slightly horrified and hoped that looks did not equate with racing ability: The foal was downright ugly. But the foal grew up to be "Count Fleet," who in 1943 won the Triple Crown and later, at stud, sired his own foal, who didn't do as well as Daddy. His name was "Count Turf," and he succeeded only in winning the Kentucky Derby in 1951.

Another pedigree conundrum was detailed by author Jim Bolus in his book *Run for the Roses: 100 Years at the Kentucky Derby*. One of the 1961 contenders, Bolus said, 'Carry Back' was not a classically bred racehorse. He was by 'Saggy' out of 'Joppa,' which didn't figure to produce anything faster than a jalopy.

But this jalopy was to mount one of the greatest comebacks in Derby history. Indeed, someone said: "He didn't start his drive to the wire at Churchill Downs. He was so far back it was like he started on the Ohio border—and won."

Another thing is that just because a mare comes forth with Man o' War one year (a mare's pregnancy is normally eleven months) doesn't mean that each time she gives birth, all the foals will be about the same quality. An old-time horseman named Ogden Phipps experienced this truth. In 1969, Christopher Chenery, who owned Meadow Stud stables, had an arrangement with Phipps, who owned Claiborne Farms. Chenery could not afford the considerable breeding fee of Derby winner "Bold Ruler" standing at stud for Claiborne, so he made an agreement that every two years, Phipps would take one of the foals sired by Bold Ruler for Chenery as payment. This continued for years. After Chenery died in 1967, his daughter, Penny Chenery, who took over Meadow Stud, was not too impressed with the arrangement and was thinking about canceling it. But she didn't, and in 1969, she and Phipps flipped a fifty-cent piece to decide who would get first foal out of the particular mare, whose name was "Something Royal." Phipps won the toss, so he got the first foal, a filly named "The Bride," who in 1971 was in four races and never finished higher than sixth. The loser, Penny Chenery, got the second foal. His name was "Secretariat," one of the greatest racehorses who ever lived. What Hall of Fame trainer Allen Jerkens said about Thoroughbred horse racing applies equally to what one will get in terms of pedigree: "The only thing you know for certain is that you know nothing for certain."

But there's another fact: The odds of getting a better racehorse are much better if you pay attention to pedigree than not. The thoroughbred racehorse is a very special horse, capable of going at speeds of up to 40 miles an hour for two minutes or more, a great feat of endurance. But it didn't get to that level of achievement by Darwinian action, at least not wholly. Man did it, breeding horses to develop a variety of characteristics, but mainly speed and endurance. There are thoroughbred horses throughout the world, but the American Thoroughbred actually started in England, about 300 years ago, with three horses known as the "Foundation Sires." They were the "Darley Arabian," the "Godolphin Arabian," and the "Byerly Turk," each named after their respective owners—Thomas Darley, Lord Godolphin, and Captain Robert Byerly—who imported the horses from the Mediterranean Middle East round the turn of the 17th century. These very three horses were bred to the stronger horse native to England and produced a breed of horse called the "thoroughbred," a horse with speed and stamina who averages about 1,000 pounds, is 16 hands high, and whose appearance reveals its Arabian ancestry. Eventually, some of these thoroughbreds were taken across the ocean to America and raced. And here's the key: Breeders kept records of how these horses performed, and before investing what might be megabucks, the potential buyer would examine these records, and more often than not, those horses with racing stars in their genealogy would be racing stars themselves. And there's a place to look. In America, for 300 years now, the pedigree of thoroughbreds has been kept by the Jockey Club of America. It keeps books on hundreds of thousands of thoroughbreds and, each year, on the 55,000 or so that are foaled.

If you are breeding horses yourself, it all boils down to mating—or "breeding," as they say in the trade—the right mare to the right sire, the idea being to produce the best possible horse.

Roy and Gretchen Jackson, who have been breeding horses, as mentioned earlier, for over 30 years, know, as you can imagine, a heck of a lot about breeding horses. But as knowledgeable as the Jacksons are about horses, breeding the right horses to produce a champion is a job for professional breeders, people who spend their lives studying horses and their pedigrees and then give educated, informed recommendations to horse owners on what might work out to produce that championship horse.

As it happened, the Jacksons had around 15 mares when they brought in an adviser named Headley Bell, a man of real pedigree himself. He is president of Nicoma Blood Stock at Mill Ridge Farm in Lexington, and he is a fifth-generation breeder. His mother, Alice Chandler, bred a horse named "Sir Ivor" who won the prestigious Epsom Derby—England's version of the Kentucky Derby—in 1968, and she also raised "Giacomo," the 2005 Kentucky Derby winner, a 50–1 shot in a race where it might have been advisable for people with heart conditions not to watch. When he was a foal he won another race, this one against death, surviving an outbreak of "mare reproductive syndrome" which destroyed 25 percent of the foals of his brood that year.

Bell met the Jacksons in the fall of 2001, and he looked at the mares in terms of their race records and pedigree (discussed above) to try to produce a championship colt. It is not a simple process. Indeed, to the uninitiated it seems about as easy to understand as nuclear fission, but out of it came their number-one candidate, "La Ville Rouge," a mid-size—not quite 16 hands

Barbaro, he even looks a little like his mom

high—mare who had what Bell said were good "pedigree blends"— ingredients from forebears that he was looking for to make a good racehorse—and had also raced well herself.

Then Bell and the Jacksons—they "contributed to every decision made," Bell said—looked for a stallion who could provide what were the missing ingredients needed in terms of physical attributes to a colt, one of which was size. For a sire they selected a large horse named "Dynaformer."

The result, of course, was Barbaro, and on paper at least it looked like he inherited the right stuff. His sire, Dynaformer, was an 11-year-old graded stakes winner who in 2003 was the top sire of grade 1 (races featuring the best horses) stakes winners such as "Riskaverse" and "Perfect Drift." Dynaformer is the son of Roberto, an English champion who has also produced such greats as

Another view of Barbaro's mom, La Ville Rouge

Sunshine Forever. Dynaformer's dam (mother) is Andover's Way, a grade 1 winner in the United States who went to the winner's circle nine times in 18 starts over two years of racing. (See chart of Barbaro's Pedigree, below.)

PEDIGREE OF BARBARO

		Hail To Reason br. 1958	Turn-To
			Nothirdchance
	Roberto b. 1969		
		Bramalea dk. b/br. 1959	Nashua
			Rarelea
Sire Dynaformer dk. b/br. 1985			
		His Majesty b. 1968	Ribot
			Flower Bowl
	Andover Way dk. b/br. 1978		
		On The Trail b. 1964	Olympia
			Golden Trail
		Mr. Prospector b. 1970	Raise A Native
			Gold Digger
	Carson City ch. 1987		
		Blushing Promise b. 1982	Blushing Groom
			Summertime Promise
Dam La Ville Rouge b. 1996			
		King's Bishop b. 1969	Round Table
			Spearfish
	La Reine Rouge b. 1978		
		Silver Betsy b. 1971	Nearctic
			Silver Abbey

"It's all a team effort," he says. "After me the Jacksons would bring the mare to the sire at another place where the covering would occur, and hopefully a live foal would be born and raised and then would be shipped to another place where it would be broken to the saddle and taught some other things and then it would be trained to race."

A live foal is something far less frequent in horses than in humans. But the determination of some mares to bring forth a live baby can be astonishing, something that few humans would endure. Take, for example, "Genuine Risk," the filly who won the 1980 Kentucky Derby in 2:02 retired after 15 starts, winning ten times and with three seconds. Then she was put out to breeding and encountered difficulties that would probably have killed anyone but a champion like her. She was bred to Secretariat first, and then to many, many other horses, and didn't give birth to a living foal until she was *sixteen years old.*

"She was," one of her grooms once said, "a champion in more ways than one."

Headley Bell is a modest—particularly for someone who suggested a pairing that resulted in a Derby winner—low-key man, and he is the first to admit that pedigree blends, or anything else, for that matter, will not absolutely produce a champion. But at least on paper, the foal born to Dynaformer and La Ville Rouge had the stuff of champions in him. It remained to be seen, of course, just how he would perform.

A Foal Is Born

*I*n a foaling barn, every night is a surprise," says Bill Sanborn, now the general manager of the 1,000-acre Wimbledon Farm in Lexington, Kentucky, but who operated the 250-acre, four-barn Sanborn Chase Farm in Nicholasville, Kentucky, the day—or rather the night—Barbaro was born. "When a mare goes down to foal, I still get a knot in my stomach. You never know what's going to happen. But if the knot ever goes away, I'm going to be in trouble."

Sanborn's wife, Sandy, is always there to help Sanborn, and the "crash kit" she carries to every foaling is indicative of the kind of serious business foaling is—and the kinds of things that can go wrong with the mare and foal. She has painkilling drugs to handle a mare in great pain, tranquilizers for one that is "fretted" out, and drugs for foals who are born with breathing problems or weak or even no heartbeat.

"If there is a problem," Sanborn says, "we have to handle it. We couldn't get a vet there fast enough."

He says that in 30 years in a breeding shed "I only needed a crash kit three times. The first time I didn't have one, and I vowed that I would always have one after that. And I did the second and third times. One of those times the foal was apparently born dead. But we were able to bring it back with the crash kit."

At Sanborn Chase and other places where he's worked, there is a 24-hour watch on the mares, particularly ones who are about to drop. "We have to watch them closely," Sanborn said. "You wouldn't want to not be around when a foal worth, say, $300,000 is born."

In the case of Barbaro, Sanborn's longtime night watchman, Irvin White, made the call in the wee hours of the morning of April 29, 2003, to the Sanborn house—which was only about 100 yards away from the foaling barn—that La Ville Rouge had broken her water. Sanborn and his wife, Sandy, crash kit in hand, made it quickly to the foaling barn.

There was nothing horrible that greeted Sanborn and his wife, but there was a slight problem. The forelegs of the foal were out of the mare in a normal fashion, but La Ville Rouge was having trouble pushing her baby out the rest of the way simply because he was very big. So Sanborn grabbed one leg and White the other . . . and together they pulled the 2006 Kentucky Derby winner into the world.

The foal was fine, and after about an hour, his mother licking him continuously, he stood up.

At first, Barbaro wasn't called "Barbaro." Everyone on the farm called him by his mother's first name, "La Ville." Later, the Jacksons dubbed him "Barbaro." Gretchen Jackson said he was named after one of six foxhounds identified in a family heirloom painting that hangs in their West Grove, Pennsylvania, home.

"The painting belonged to my husband's grandfather," she said, "and, below each head, each one is identified. Barbaro is one of the cuter hounds in the painting."

"We have found no known origin of the picture," she added, "but it has always been a favorite of ours since it was discovered."

The birth of Barbaro at Sanborn Chase was just another step, as mentioned earlier by Headley Bell, in an overall plan the Jacksons and their connections had created to raise their foals into champion racehorses. Headley Bell had given them the advice, as mentioned in chapter 1, on whom to mate: The dam would be La Ville Rouge and the sire should be Dynaformer. Sanborn and his team had arranged for and supervised the covering. The usual procedure at Sanborn Chase was for the mare to go to the stallion. First, though, the mare is "teased" by a "teaser stallion" to make sure she is in heat, this indicated, among other things, by her vulva opening and closing (known in the trade as "winking") raising her tail, and showing interest in the stallion. As a final precaution, to make sure she is in heat, a vet palpates her ovaries.

Once at the breeding shed, the people there will tease her again to make sure she's in heat, and then breeding will occur.

The actual breeding speed depends on the horse. Sanborn says one of the slowest breeders he ever knew was "Seattle Slew." "He was bred outside, and if a bird flew by he would be distracted and lose track of what he wanted to do. But he was one of the most fertile horses I ever knew of. We had mares that didn't ovulate after they were bred for four to five days and he would still get them in foal. He was incredibly fertile."

In the case of Dynaformer and La Ville Rouge, breeding was normal. Sanborn says that the whole thing took about two hours, which included traveling back and forth between Sanborn Chase and the breeding shed.

Sanborn Chase took care of La Ville Rouge throughout her pregnancy. Now that Barbaro was born, Sanborn and his team were also responsible for him—and lots of other mares and foals on the property.

And there is no question that being responsible for a thoroughbred foal is a big responsibility, and takes a lot of TLC—just like children do. "It's a twenty-four/seven job," Sanborn says. "You spend more time with horses more than your children."

The foal's health is key. "The day after he was born," Sanborn says, "blood was drawn to make sure he was okay and he was given five days of antibiotics to ward off disease."

Rather quickly, too, he is led into the pasture, and what he's doing is constantly monitored. What he's doing can make a horsemen's belly go a little hollow. Running with other colts, playing, there's always the possibility of the colt getting hurt. But Sanborn obviously agrees with the philosophy that more than one sailor has uttered: "A ship will be safe if it stays in port, but that's not what it was built for." Says Sanborn: "It makes you worry, but to me, it's the best way [letting them run free] to raise them, you'll have a lot less stall vices [bad habits developed when a horse spends too much time in a stall], and vices period, if you can keep them [the young horses] together. Because once you separate them out, you're the only playmate they've got."

At one point Barbaro did get hurt. He hit a leg in the pasture and developed a "splint"—a small but painful bony enlargement. The injury required him to be stall-bound for two weeks while the farm staff treated him with cold hosing and bandaging. But it turned out well.

As he grew, the horsemen on the farm automatically compared him with the other colts, and though he always seemed to be a leader and faster, that didn't tell anyone that he would grow up to be a superstar. (Indeed, there are numerous examples of horsemen not knowing what they had until the derby had been run!) Says watchman Irvin White, "He was always different from the rest. I always thought he'd go on to the races and do well, but I never knew he'd do this!"

Horses can have widely varying personalities, some of them downright nasty. This can affect the way they are trained, but it would be a mistake to assume that nastiness or any other personality trait automatically translated into speed and endurance. It doesn't.

Whatever, Barbaro had a wonderful, warm personality, and everyone at Sanborn Chase liked and even loved him. Keith Ritchie, a man who worked in the foaling barn and proudly and smilingly claims to be one of the earliest viewers of Barbaro, said, "The first time I saw him was on a fourteen-day pregnancy scan on the ultra-sound," Ritchie says. "I say I knew him since he was a follicle."

"And," Ritchie continues, "he was so mild-mannered, I could roll him over on his back and scratch his belly [a very vulnerable position for an animal] or pick out his feet," he said. "He was big, but he wasn't lanky. He was real brawny. And he had the nicest temperament."

Sally Mullis, who also worked in the foaling barn, describes Barbaro as a model student with a laid-back personality, what might be known in human circles as a "good boy." "To me," she says, "he was just a nice little bay colt." "He chimed right in and got with the program. He was not a troublemaker."

"On ESPN on derby morning," Sanborn said, "they showed him standing there with his head hanging and that lower lip flapping, and I said, 'There he is.' He was always like that. You'd walk by him, pat him on the head, and say, 'Hey, La Ville, how you doing, boy?' He just liked to watch things. He was a cool horse. It never bothered him to be confined to a stall, and that's a pretty neat personality."

Barbaro grew not in millimeters but spurts. "When he hit a growth spurt, they were big growth spurts," Sanborn says. "His elbows would stick out—all of a sudden. Then he'd stop growing and develop out, and everything looked fine again."

Some owners have horses raised for them with a quick payday strictly in mind. The horses are raised and then sold. But the horses of the Jacksons were not for sale. And Sanborn liked it that way.

"It was nice raising horses for the Jacksons because none of their horses were sales horses," Sanborn said. "We'd run them with the sales horses until it was time to separate the sales horses out, and we could leave the Jacksons' horses together with other horses. But you'd watch them go out and they're all rearing and jumping on each other, and you think, 'Oh my God, he's going to hit a knee.' "

Though, as mentioned, no one claims to have seen Barbaro as a future Kentucky Derby winner, Bill Sanborn said he did see "a race mind," a kind of focus that racehorses have. And despite Barbaro's great personality, he did have what old-time breeders call the "look of eagles" in his eyes. For example, the original path of 1992 Kentucky Derby winner "Lil E. Tee" as a racehorse was an odyssey to nowhere—small races in small towns and then good-bye. Louis Littmann, his owner and breeder at Pin Oak Lane Farm in Pennsylvania, put him up for sale at the age of two for a whopping $3,000. But one highly astute horse trainer, Chuck Weinike, who made his living taking horses off the scrap heap and turning them into salable merchandise, saw something he liked. To Weinike he was like a big, rawboned teenager. Weinike figured if he could fill him out, the horse could well be worth something. Maybe he could get $20,000 for him.

Months later, when Weinike sold him, Lil E. Tee had filled out, and he got $25,000 and one of the bidders, Bill McGreevy, who had lost out on the sale to a man named Al Jevromovic, was very upset because he had seen in Lil E. Tee's eyes the "look of eagles." Knowing. Confident. Fierce. The look of a winner. And later, McGreevey learned he had been just one $1,000 bid away from getting him.

"But again," says Sanborn, echoing other horsemen, "you could never tell how far he—or any other colt—would go."

Barbaro was weaned from his mother in five months. "He stayed in a stall that had a mesh door," Sanborn says, "that was specially made with a diamond cut out of it, where a horse could put his head out. Even as a baby, he liked to keep his head out."

Barbaro stayed at Sanborn Chase until the fall of 2004, when he was a little over a year old, and the crew at Sanborn Chase bid "La Ville" adieu, as it were, and then he would be shipped to a horse farm for some basic training, and then to his trainer, who would train him to race.

No question that Sanborn and other horsemen at the farm felt a sense of loss when Barbaro left. But of course, it would not be the final time Sanborn would see little "La Ville." That was May 6, 2006, a day to remember.

Sanborn was happy for the patient trainer, Michael Matz. "This horse is so big and so fast, the tendency would be to pull the trigger too fast and too often," Sanborn says. "Matz resisted the urge."

And he was happy for Roy and Gretchen Jackson. "They've been clients of mine for years," Sanborn says. "They're first-class people with top-notch broodmares, and they deserve this."

And he was happy for himself. Once, a Sanborn-trained colt had come close to winning the Derby. In 1984, while he was working at Catawba Farm in Lexington, Sanborn helped develop a colt named "Coax Me Chad" who, with Herb McCauley up, would go on to run second in the Derby to "Swale." But second wasn't first. "I was ecstatic."

And that ever-present horseman in him just loved what he saw.

"It was breathtaking to see that horse win the way he did," Sanborn says, still not over it. "He was hand-ridden to the wire. It was like he was asking [Edgar] Prado, 'How fast do you want me to go?' "

And it is not too far a stretch to think that Sanborn was also feeling the pride a father might feel about seeing his son achieve something glorious. Because, no question, some of what was imprinted in Barbaro at Sanborn Chase was inside him when he burst out of the pack and electrified the crowd as he roared to a 6½-length Derby victory, the biggest in over 60 years. No question at all.

*Abruptly the plane started making
terrifying leaps upward . . .*
—**Tom Philbin and Pamela K. Brodowsky**

The Man Who
Saved Their
Childhood—
and Them

On July 19, 1989, United Airlines flight
232, a DC-10 with 285 passengers and
eight crew aboard, lifted off from Staple-
ton Airport in Denver bound for Philadelphia.

Sometime after the plane left Staple-
ton, what was later characterized as a
one-in-a-billion event occurred. A fan
disk on the single-engine plane cracked

3

and pieces of metal sprayed inside the engine housing and sliced through all three of the plane's redundant—for safety—hydraulic cables, the system that basically allowed the pilots to control the up, down, and side-to-side movements of the aircraft. Abruptly the plane started making terrifying leaps upward, and then equally terrifying and precipitous drops downward, losing about 1,500 feet every time it dropped. Inside the cockpit, the pilots tried desperately to bring some measure of control to the plane.

The passengers, of course, were screaming, terrified, traumatized.

A wiry, angular man was sitting in one of the middle rows, and sitting next to him were two little boys who were brothers, Travis and Jody Roth; a couple of rows away was their sister, Melissa Radcliffe.

The world around him falling apart, the man immediately flashed his brilliant big-toothed grin and launched into a reassuring "rap" to the scared children about how everything was fine and would be all right. The kids listened and believed him, but of course everything was not all right. In fact, there was a good possibility everyone on the plane would end up dead. But he kept talking and smiling, and the children later said that he calmed them, that he created childhood illusions in which they were safe.

The pilots succeeded in getting the plane in some measure of control. The captain, Al Haynes, found out that by accelerating and decelerating the remaining engine, the pilots could keep the plane moving forward in the direction they wanted, which was toward the closest airport where they could land—if they could land—in Sioux City, Iowa. As they approached the airport, the pilots were in continuous radio contact with the control tower, and they were told to put down on a 9,000-foot runway—almost two miles long—which should be more than long enough to land. On an adjacent runway, safety trucks, ambulances, and all the other rescue gear and personnel would be waiting, watching the sky, ready to spring into action as soon as the plane came to a stop.

And as they approached, closer to what one person characterized as a "showdown with the ground," the wiry man continued to reassure the kids.

But then, with the airport precariously close—came a new terror. The pilots realized they could not control the plane well enough to land on the 9,000-foot runway, that they would have to put it down on the much shorter adjacent runway—where rescue teams and equipment waited! Barking their predicament to the control tower, the pilots made, for lack of a better word, what could be described as a "landing."

As it happened, TV crews were on hand, and the landing was captured and is famous—or infamous. It basically shows the plane hurtling along the runway and then turning from a plane into a fireball. It did not look like anyone would survive.

It continued until it turned over and plowed, upside down, into an adjacent cornfield. The man and the children were still in their seat belts. They released themselves. He told them to grab his pants belt from behind. They—and their sister, who had joined them—did, and the man led them through the smoky wreckage out a hole in the fuselage. One of the children, Melissa, said that she will "never forget the smoke and dust and darkness" and the reassuring voice of the man.

"Outside," Melissa said, "he told us to run through the adjacent cornfield. "Run away and don't look back," Melissa says. "So the three of us ran, holding hands."

But the man's heroics were not over. As he had made his way through the plane to safety, at one point he had heard a baby crying. So outside, completely safe, he chose to go back into the plane and then also found the baby in an overhead rack and carried it to safety.

The man who saved the three children and the baby was Michael Matz, now 55, the man who was to train Barbaro. And he had saved more than their lives. He had saved, they said later, their childhood illusions that they lived in a perfectly safe world where everything always turned out right. They believed that because the man told them so.

Matz's story, like those of so many great people in horse racing, was motivated by one thing: his love of horses.

In the beginning, though, he didn't even know horses, and if he had not told a fib he might never had known. It was a fluke.

Matz was raised in Shillington, Pennsylvania, a small town near Reading, and as a young man had gotten a job with a neighbor doing various things on his property. Then one day the neighbor asked him a question:

"Do you know how to ride a horse? I'd like someone to ride with me."

Matz didn't, but he had the feeling that to keep his job he had to say yes.

"Sure," he said, "I can ride."

So he started to ride with his neighbor, and he found—eureka—that he could ride. He took to it naturally, and gradually, he also started to love horses. Indeed, while he attended the local

Michael Matz

Albright College, he found himself distracted, staring out the window, daydreaming about a life that included him being a horseman. He had come down with that severe malady, equine addiction.

At one point, he considered trying to be a jockey, but though wiry and slim, he was not small enough, so he would have to find something else.

So one day he set out to do just that.

"I left home with a sleeping bag," he said. He traveled around to horse shows, where he could get jobs working with and on horses, and he didn't worry about the sleeping accommodations. "I asked where I'd stay, and they pointed to a bale of hay in the barn. . . . I loved the horses, so I didn't mind."

His travels to various horse shows enabled him to learn about horses from, as it were, the hoof up. "I was getting experience, traveling to horse shows, and still making money."

And when he rode show horses he was spotted as being good—very good.

"A natural. Great athlete, great balance," says trainer Tim Ritchey, a former steeplechase rider who trained "Afleet Alex" to wins in the Preakness and Belmont Stakes.

By 1973, Matz was a full-fledged pro, and he entered show-horse competitions in Europe. Then, in 1976, he tried out for and snared a birth with the U.S. Olympic Equestrian team that went to Montreal. He was filled with confidence; in fact, overconfidence.

"I didn't even go to the opening ceremony because I said, 'I'll do this every four years.' Well, it took me sixteen years to get back, and when I did, I was the first one on the bus. You learn about things, not to take them as for sure."

Over the years, Matz had great success as a show jumper. He compiled the highest amount of winnings—$1,700,000—ever in show jumping. He is a two-time winner of the American Grandprix Association's Rider of the Year (1981 and 1984) and won five goal medals over the years at the Pan American Games. He was also on the Olympic show-jumping team in 1996 and won a second-place silver medal and was voted by the U.S. Olympic team to lead the entire team in the closing ceremonies, not only because he epitomized the ideal U.S. athlete at the games but because of his acts of heroism in 1989. He is now a member of the Show Jumping Hall of Fame.

In 1998, since he knew so much about horses, Matz started to train a few thoroughbreds in his spare time. Then, in 2000, he tried out again for the U.S. Olympic show-jumping team, but this time he didn't make it. It was time to hang up the bridle—at least when it came to show jumping.

But what he didn't lose, of course, was his love of horses. He decided to turn to thoroughbred training full-time. It didn't matter that the horses he was involved with ran on a flat surface rather than leaping up and gliding over barriers. As in the old TV show *Mr. Ed,* Matz's song was the same . . . "A horse is a horse, of course, of course . . ."

It wasn't exactly a triumphant transition. As the leading money winner in jumping, he was treated with great respect, almost as if he were royalty. Then he was no longer king; he was more like a serf.

"I went from here to down here," he said, raising a hand above his head, then lowering it to his ankle. "Nobody wanted to give you stalls because you didn't have a reputation." He was in the classic catch-22 situation, but gradually he did get a stall and for a simple reason: He is a person of the highest quality—a hero, a champion in every way—and it doesn't take long before his character is shining through as brightly as his incandescent smile.

Matz certainly had picked the right helper when he got into training thoroughbreds. He had married fellow show rider Alexandra Kleberg—in fact, she survived the plane crash with him—who had been born into equine royalty. Alexandra, or "D-D," is a granddaughter of Robert J. Kleberg of King Ranch in Kingsville, Texas. The mammoth one-million-acre (or maybe now only 875,000 acres) spread was the breeding ground for 1946 Triple Crown winner Assault, or the "Clubfoot Comet," the first horse from Texas to win a Derby (by 8 lengths), no less a Triple Crown. Assault's trainer was Max Hirsch, one of the best trainers of all time, and D-D had picked up quite a few tidbits that she could relay to her husband and was able to help him greatly in his new pursuits—and then some. In fact she probably knew more than he did about training thoroughbreds.

As with any life, however, it has not been all bliss for the Matzes. While they had four children, ages three to nine, and two others from Matz's previous marriage, at one point D-D was diagnosed with thyroid cancer, but she survived it. "It was a rough time, but everything's all right," Matz said.

Gretchen and Roy Jackson, who were constantly expanding their Lael Farms Stable, were looking for a trainer, and one day their paths crossed Michael Matz's. They spotted him competing while they were attending a horse show in Devon, Pennsylvania. "And he had an impeccable reputation as a horseman," said Gretchen Jackson. "He was the picture of perfection. We just knew he'd make a perfect trainer for some of our horses."

They started sending him horses, and he did a very good job. More horses led to more horses and to a growing reputation in the area where he operated around Elkton, Maryland.

Training thoroughbreds, he found, has at least one big drawback. Having ridden for so many years, if he had a problem with a show-jumping horse, Matz could simply climb astride the horse and, through "feel," diagnose what the problem was out of his own experience. But he's not a jockey, so he can't do that with his thoroughbreds and has to depend on the jockey to tell him what, if anything, is wrong. "It makes you a little nervous, especially when they [the jockeys] don't speak English very well," he said. "But I don't like to tell them too much. You just know there has to be a connection between the rider and the horse, and there's not much more you can do."

Matz continued to be very successful as a trainer. This is because, says horsewomen Sally Ike, "he's meticulous, committed to excellence and to the highest standards. And he doesn't compromise." In a word, he's a perfectionist.

For example, a couple of years ago, Sally and a friend visited Matz at his Palm Meadows stable in Boynton Beach, Florida. Sally says: "The stable was spotless, not a thing out of place. We walked around the shed row, and he knew everything about every horse and their breeding and what the plans for them were. It was an incredibly well-oiled machine. His whole operation just transferred from jumping to racing. At the end of the day, that's why he's where he is. A stickler for detail."

Matz garnered his first grade 1 victory as a trainer of throughbreds with "Kricken Kris," who snared the 2003 Secretariat Stakes and the 2004 Arlington Million, the latter via disqualification. That was a great thrill for Matz, but perhaps not unexpected. He had been a winner as a show jumper, and he would be a winner training thoroughbreds.

Different trainers train thoroughbreds differently. Michael Matz, of course, had his own way to train Barbaro, the core of which, as it turned out, was quite controversial, and a lot of pressure was put on him to change it. In the end, though, he didn't. He might have been wrong. But he had the courage of his convictions. And on Derby Day it surely didn't seem that way.

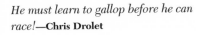

He must learn to gallop before he can race!—**Chris Drolet**

Training Barbaro

4

*I*t's surprising to think of it, but a thoroughbred racehorse must be taught how to gallop around a track. Or as horsewoman Chris Drolet couched it facetiously: "He must learn to gallop before he can race!" Galloping is not a thoroughbred's natural gait. Also, if there were no track training involved, all horses might end up where 1942 superstar

Whirlaway—Gretchen Jackson's favorite horse when she was a little girl—was. He would start running around the track, then simply veer off and go hell-bent-for-leather for the outside rail, then start running along it. Of course Whirlaway was so fast that he could win the race even if he ran next to the outside rail. "But it's not recommended!" says Drolet.

Before he was given to anyone for final racetrack training, galloping him was just one of a number of basic things Barbaro—and any racehorse, for that matter—has to be taught. And for this basic training he was shipped from Sanborn Chase to Stephenson Thoroughbreds in Morriston, Florida, a 110-acre facility with three training barns, 70 stalls, and a 6-furlong track run, surrounded by woods where he was to learn some basic things related to racing and worked out so he got strong. The facility is owned by a couple in their 40s named John and Jill Stephenson. They have been training horses for quite a long time, but only on their own since 1998 and for the Jacksons for five years. At any given time there might be 80 to 100 young thoroughbreds on the property, which is located in the Ocala area. And one thing is abundantly clear: The area cannot have a finger wagged at it for being unlucky. The last three Kentucky Derby winners—"Giacomo," 2005; "Smarty Jones," 2004; "and "Funny Cide," 2003—as well as Barbaro, got their basic training in facilities there!

Another part of this basic training regimen is getting a saddle and rider on the horse, and this must be done with slow, surgical precision. If a horse has a rough or bad experience, some future rider may find him- or herself going aloft, propelled there by a horse who was never "broken" properly.

Jill and John Stephenson take great pains to give individual horses personal attention, so just how long this process takes will vary depending on the horse, but in general it takes about a month.

One overall thing the trainer has to do during breaking—as well as other training—is to keep calm. To do this, one has to look at the world through the young horse's eyes and be aware how the horse is exposed to new sights, sounds, feelings, and expectations. For example, breaking might start with allowing the horse to smell the saddle cloth before anyone even attempts to place it on his back. It is also a slow process placing a saddle on the horse's back, and, of course, it takes a bit of time for a rider to finally climb up and sit on—and ride—the horse.

Another thing Barbaro learned at the Stephenson's was how to break from a starting gate, a process that has to be done very carefully. If you think about it, this would not necessarily come naturally. And it can be dangerous, as indicated a few years ago by an incident that occurred involving Smarty Jones, an eventual Kentucky Derby winner. In July 2003, trainer John Servis was hired to train him. That same year, Servis was teaching Smarty the ins and outs of the starting gate when suddenly Smarty reared up and smashed his head up into the top of the gate, which made him fall in a heap, blood pouring from his nostrils. At first Servis thought he was dead, but he wasn't, though he almost lost the sight of one eye. (Ironically, in the Derby he ran in, there were two one-eyed horses.)

Horses' personalities can count heavily when problematic because they can give a trainer real problems. For example, "Omaha," one of the favorites in the 1935 Run for the Roses, had a secret, and his owner, William Woodard, his jockey Willie "Smokey"

Saunders, and his exercise rider were terrified that others would find out, because if they did it could result in the big horse being lured into a trap that would eliminate him from the race.

Saunders had discovered the problem during a workout.

"They used to work two horses with him," Saunders said. "They'd work a horse the first half mile, and then they'd bring another horse in with him, and they broke this horse off the outside fence to hook in with him and didn't get him straightened out fast enough and brushed Omaha when he came in." And what does Omaha do? He stops and bites the other horse. And he could do that again, so all someone would have to do was bring another horse in there to bump Omaha and get him fighting—not running. "Naturally," Saunders said, "I was very cautious. That's why I always had to take him around horses, rather than take a chance on a horse hitting him."

But Barbaro gave no such problems. "He was a very nice horse," said John Stephenson.

And how did he feel about Barbaro's chances of becoming a good racehorse? "We definitely thought he'd be a very good racehorse, but there's no way you can tell if a horse is going to go on to be a great horse."

In fact, horsemen will tell you that no one can tell, not even when a horse is at the starting gate in the Derby.

Jill and John worked Barbaro well, but at what they perceived was his own pace.

"It's all about giving a horse time to develop," said Stephenson. "Our program is very geared toward the individual. Our clients race, so there's no pressure to get a horse ready for the juvenile sales. It is how we like to operate."

But one of their main goals, too, was to make sure that Barbaro was developing well physically, and Jill particularly would take him out on long jaunts to build up his strength and stamina.

By the spring of 2005, Barbaro was ready to be shipped to the trainer who would, in the words of horsewoman Chris Drolet, "racetrack-train him to accomplish one thing: run faster than other horses most—if not all—of the time." And toward that end the trainers' influence is pervasive. They devise and implement the training program, select the jockey, devise race-day strategy—because they know the horse best—and often are the difference between winning and losing. For example, in the 1940 Derby "Bimelech's" regular trainer, "Derby Dick" Thompson, had passed away and a new trainer named Bill Hurley was hired to train him. Hurley, it was said, didn't train Bimelech hard enough, only starting to train him in the early spring before the derby, and then he ran him in two races that were very close to the Derby—the Blue Grass Stakes and the Derby trials—two days later, and analysts say that it tired the horse terribly and "Gallahadion" won. The final assessment was that Hurley had left what could have been a winning derby run on the tracks of those pre-Derby races.

And a trainer like Ben A. Jones—one of the greatest trainers who ever lived—not only made a difference in terms of horses that won races but also made a difference to a stable that survived because of him. In the early 1940s, starting with Whirlaway, Jones had so many winners, Calumet Farms, who employed him, did quite well. Indeed, it was considered the greatest stable of its time. But when Jones went out of the picture in the '50s, Calumet started a slide of no winners that ultimately was a big factor in its going bankrupt.

Trainers take different routes to make a thoroughbred run fast, but overall it's usually based on their perception of what distance the individual horse runs best and its styles. The horse might be a sprinter, like to come from way off the pace, or might like to lead, for example. But some trainers are quite unusual. A candidate for the most unusual was Juan Arias, a small chain-smoking black man and the trainer of "Canonero II," who ran in the 1971 Kentucky Derby, Preakness, and Belmont Stakes. Horsemen who observed Arias and his contingent, who were from Caracas, Venezuela, regarded them as strange, more than a little eccentric. For example, the horse was a little odd looking. He was normal looking in almost every way, except his forelock—the hair that hangs down on the forehead—was cut in bangs, and one horsemen commented that it made him look like "Moe of the Three Stooges."

Arias was a little strange himself, very emotional, a man who had been raised in the slums of Caracas and had escaped into what he considered the beautiful world of horse racing, and he was always dressed in a suit and tie, even in the stable, and approached his horse not as a horse but a beloved son. Arias was a loving, indulgent father, someone quite the opposite of the father who had abandoned him. He petted Canonero, hugged him, kissed him—and acted on what the horse "said." That is, Arias would ask Canonero (he was named Canonero II because another horse had been named Canonero), say, if he felt like working, and Canonero would answer him "yes" or "no" or maybe "sí" or "no" (Arias didn't say what language the horse used). And Arias was also not adverse to running him slowly, when Canonero told him that's how he wanted to run that day. Very slowly. The first time Canonero ran in

Lexington, for example, after a torturous trip from Caracas that featured him standing in a hot stable for 24 hours to get the necessary bloodwork done and facing a 12-hour trip to Lexington by truck instead of plane—he covered a half mile in a turtlelike 53 and ⅗ seconds.

But a few days before the Derby, Arias explained—and exclaimed: "Most of the American trainers train for speed. I train Canonero to be a star, a horse of depth who is versatile and can be ridden in front or from behind. They say my horse is too slow. Let's see if he runs that slow on Saturday."

Arias stuck to his methods and made a simple statement that reiterated his beliefs on Derby Day: "Nobody knows my horse. But after today the world will know him."

He was right. Canonero II won the Derby by 3¾ lengths as well as the Preakness, and it is said that he would have won the Belmont Stakes but was sick when that race occurred. And from that time on he was known not as Canonero II but as "The Caracas Cannonball."

In the spring of 2005, Barbaro was shipped from Stephenson Thoroughbreds to someone who would also come to be regarded as a very unusual trainer—Michael Matz at Fair Hill Training Center in Elkton, Maryland. And from day one, Matz and his exercise trainer, a British ex-jockey named Peter Brette, were impressed with the dark bay colt. Both started to think about the Kentucky Derby . . . and beyond.

The core of Matz's training of Barbaro—which was considered unusual and suspect by some other horsemen—was not to overtrain the horse, which included not racing him frequently.

Matz said he had learned that bitter lesson in the Olympics: "In

Peter Brette, Barbaro's main exercise rider

1976, I rode in the Olympics, and the whole team was fighting to see who would ride in that last spot." So he exercised and exercised his horse. And "when we finally got to the Olympics, I had no horse left. So I said from that day that whatever I do, whatever competition I go into, I want to make sure I can be competitive, and that requires a fresh horse. I certainly want to come into a race with a horse that's fresh and hasn't raced too much. That was the whole plan [with Barbaro] from the very beginning."

And he did, even though the media would quote unnamed sources leveling carping criticism at him for not working the horse enough. His exercise rider, Peter Brette, who loved Barbaro, would work him out briskly, but never to the point of exhaustion.

For his part, Matz was not sweating much as he trained Barbaro, because he feels it's not he who's devising and imposing

Brette and Matz at Fair Hill Training Center in Elkton, Maryland, where Barbaro was trained

training on the horse but the horse who's telling him how to train him (though we doubt very much he would listen if Barbaro told him one day, say, that he did not feel like running like Canonero). Getting to know the horse, getting to know what it wants and needs is everything. And it could take time that Matz and other outstanding trainers were, of course, willing to spend. Once, for example, a person observed the great trainer Ben A. Jones standing by a fence looking at a black horse. When the man passed by again an hour later, he saw that Jones was still there.

"What you doing?" he asked Jones.

"Getting to know the horse."

And that is Matz to a T. It's all about maximizing a horse's potential, but first it's a good idea if you know what makes it tick—and run fast.

Barbaro being run at Fair Hill, Brette aboard

Some people also questioned Matz's background in show jumping as being counterproductive to training thoroughbreds. Matz did not see any profound difference between the two.

"Horsemanship," he said, "is horsemanship." The two apparently dissimilar areas, he emphasized, "are both rooted in understanding what the individual horse wants and needs. And it will tell you what it needs."

As mentioned earlier, the only potential problem is that the trainer can't get as close to the thoroughbred as he can with the show jumper.

"The difference is that with show jumpers," Matz reiterated, "I'd do the training and competing myself. Now I did—and do—everything to get the horse ready and put someone else up for the competition. I've had times when I've felt a little helpless putting the jockey up on the horse. That's frustrating."

"There are certain things," Matz said, "I took from my experience training show horses and applied to racing. I don't claim that my way is the best way; I'm still learning. When you stop learning, that's your problem."

Matz always has great demands on his time, as he did when he was training Barbaro, because he does not use the training center for training a single horse, but for many. And there is always a flow of two-year-olds coming from Stephenson Thoroughbreds. Matz, who concentrates intensely, may momentarily bristle at the various demands on his time—such as requests from the media for interviews—but he has learned to compartmentalize. "As long as they let me do my work," Matz said of all who ask something of him. Nor will he disrupt the lives of the horses. "I don't think it's fair to the horses. They need peace and quiet also."

As Barbaro's racetrack training proceeded, Matz, the Jacksons, and all their connections were developing higher and higher hopes for Barbaro. And Peter Brette had come to realize something: At one point he told Matz, "Barbaro is the best horse I've ever ridden."

As the time came closer—Barbaro was now a two-year-old—and closer to racing age, Matz had some things to decide, one of which was how long the races Barbaro was entered into should be. The length of the race could make a big difference. Some horses, as suggested earlier, are better at sprints, and some at longer races. Bill Sanborn, for example, had said once about Barbaro's dam that despite the fact that her father was strictly a sprinter, "La Ville Rouge wasn't so inclined. A mile and an eighth to a mile and a

Not all is training. Relaxation, Barbaro says, is important too.

quarter," Sanborn says, "that was her best lick." Maybe Barbaro would turn out that way. It's one thing to observe a horse in training, but racing is the acid test.

There was also the question of whether he should run on turf or dirt. The surface a horse races on can make a big difference. Most of the tracks in the country are dirt, but there are many turf surfaces, and different horses prefer different surfaces. A horse that races, say, on a dry dirt surface may do very well. Put the same horse on a muddy, sloppy dirt surface, and he won't do well—or he might do well. So-called mudders have won many big races that they were not expected to because the surface was sloppy. Also, a horse may perform well on a firm turf surface—and poorly on one that's loose.

Horses tend to perform well on one particular surface—mud,

say—and continue that way over their entire careers. Hence when handicappers look at a race, they consider the horses' past performances on the particular surface.

Usually, horses tend to slide more on dirt surfaces. The ground is looser than turf, and after the hoof hits the ground, it skids. This skidding action places severe stress on leg structures and muscles.

The action of a horse's gait also makes a difference. Horses that have high action (an up and down rather than a long and sweeping stride) will perform well on both sloppy attacks and turf, due to their ability to skip over such surfaces.

Some trainers also believe that some horses have an advantage running on some kinds of surfaces if they have big feet because they give better stability due to their "spread" over more surface and therefore "grip" it better.

Again, though, pedigree usually matters. Ever notice how you have the skills that one or both of your parents have? That's because of pedigree too, but sometimes it's because of dumb luck.

And of course, Matz had to find a good jockey to ride their good horse, who was clearly seen as having great potential. They didn't just find a "good" jockey. They found one of the greatest who ever lived.

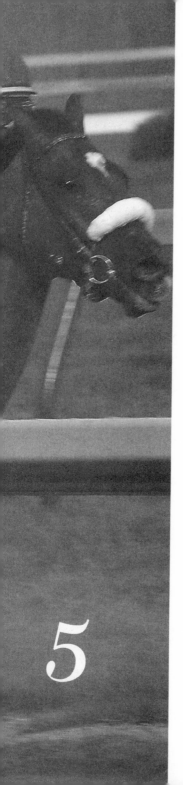

One Great Jockey

5

Paul Jones," a thoroughbred contender in the 1920 Kentucky Derby, was widely regarded as a so-so racehorse, but he had one quality that shone over all others: He had a nasty temperament. But he paid for it big-time. To improve his disposition, his owners had his testicles cut off, turning him into a gelding. It had something of a positive effect on him, but of course rendered him useless for stud service later.

Perhaps in part because of this, though, Paul Jones didn't have an affectionate or even respectful relationship with his jockeys. In his first five starts, four different jockeys rode him, but in his sixth race Ted Rice climbed on his back, and horse and man hit it off well right away. Why? Who knew. Why do we love one person and not another? It's hard to figure. Paul Jones had not won a single race in any of his starts, but with Rice piloting him he won his first race, the Bouquet Selling Stakes at Belmont Park.

As the Derby approached, Rice did fairly well with Paul Jones, winning some and losing some. And against all odds, with Rice aboard, he won the Kentucky Derby.

The object lesson implicit in the relationship of jockey and horse described above has been repeated over and over again in horse racing. Some jockeys get along with, have a strong affection or regard for some horses—and vice versa. They connect. And equally important to realize, some don't.

The ability to connect was one of the qualities that Michael Matz was looking for when they sought a jockey. Implicit in Matz's search—he did not have a checklist in hand but in his head—were certain other characteristics that he knew great jockeys shared. One was courage, or a lack of concern in a threatening racing situation. Perhaps the best way to determine this is to ask to see jockey X rays! It would be hard to find a great jockey who has not taken a fall or broken some bones, and many have broken numerous bones. For example, Jose Santos, the winning jockey who rode Funny Cide in the 2003 Kentucky Derby, had had an accident in the spring of 1992. Santos's left shoulder blade cracked when his horse fell, after one of its legs buckled; his recovery took five weeks. Then, the following July, while racing at Belmont Park in Elmont, Long Island,

New York, he was involved in a terrible accident in which his horse and two others collided and crashed to the ground with their riders. The potential for injury in such spills is huge: On average, thoroughbred horses weigh 1,100 pounds, about nine times as much as the average jockey, who tips the scales at no more than 115. (Some thoroughbreds weigh as much as 1,450 pounds.) Santos, who stands about five feet two inches and weighs 110 pounds, emerged from the Belmont collision with a broken collarbone, hip, and right arm; the repair of the arm required a graft of bone (from his undamaged hip), two pins, and 14 screws. "I stayed in bed twenty-one days in one position, I couldn't move to the side . . . ," Santos recalled to Joseph Durso for *The New York Times* (November 29, 1992). "I spent the summer watching TV and taking therapy and wondering when I'd come back." By the end of 1992, Santos resumed racing.

Angel Cordero Jr. is another great jockey who you'd need a strong stomach to look at naked. His body looks like he had met up with King Kong on a bad day.

Jockeys unflinchingly face death, of course, but sometimes their injuries can be worse than death. For example, Ron Turcotte, the Canadian jockey who rode the incomparable Secretariat—"Big Red"—to victory in under two minutes in the 1973 Derby, was thrown by a horse named "The Legend of Leyte" and was turned into a paraplegic. And the courts decided against him in his suit (it was a classic decision) against the track. The court said that Turcotte was not entitled to any damages because when he rode the horse he automatically consented to the normal hazards of his profession.

Some jockeys don't consider taking big chances as being courageous. It's not facing fear, it's a necessity to win by making the right move in a race.

Many years ago, for example, when Willie Shoemaker was asked if he was afraid—a necessary opposite to courage—when he powered his horse though an opening that was one horse wide and one misstep could kill him, he said:

"You don't think about that when you do it."

Great jockeys are highly intelligent. They must also have the ability to make quick decisions. A race is like a chess game, except the chess pieces are moving at 40 miles an hour. You see a "hole" between horses, and you move through it in seconds—or milliseconds. And if the hole closes suddenly while you're going through it, you have problems.

Additionally, great jockeys know when to make certain moves so they will have a clear run to the wire in the stretch, where most races are won or lost.

Jockeys also have a certain style of riding that Matz and other trainers factor into their decisions. Some, for example, like to pilot horses that run from the front, while others are good with horses that run from behind.

Take, for instance, Conn McCreary. When the gates clanged open, his Calumet Farms mount Pensive in the 1944 Derby quickly fell back, but this was by design—McCreary's design. He was known for holding his mounts back, then coming from far back to win.

In this race, McCreary dropped all the way back to 13th in the field of 16.

As he approached the mile marker, he started to move up to 5th on the inside. And then, boom, he started to really run, powering along next to the rail, and horses fell behind as he went past. Ironically, in the 1951 Derby he was hired by an owner to ride Count Turf because this was a horse that liked to hang back; ironic because in the jockeys' room, McCreary had heard that a number of jockeys intended to hang back and he didn't want to get lost in the crowd. He ran from the front and won.

The best jockeys have a certain something, an ability to speak to the horse so that at that certain moment when he needs the horse to run all out, he can make what lots of jockeys describe as a "clucking" sound, or rub his hands against the horse's neck or even crack the horse's flank with a whip, and the horse's afterburners go on and what might have been an also-ran is now a winner. The agent of two-time Derby winner Chris Antley, Drew Mollica, said that it also helps if you're "part horse."

Today's jockeys also can be rough in a race—trying, essentially, to intimidate other riders. But it is not as bad as it used to because now jockeys know cameras are trained on them and they must behave.

One of the roughest riders of all was Earl Sande. He was horse racing's version of Mike Tyson of boxing, or an enforcer for a pro hockey team. Nasty and ruthless, but he was also a great jockey.

In the '30s, one of the greatest jockeys who ever lived started riding, namely, George Edward "Eddie" Arcaro, who weighed in at three pounds at his birth in Cincinnati but was raised across the river in Southgate, Kentucky. Arcaro, whose generous nose eventually earned him the dubious nickname "Banana Nose," would ultimately win five Kentucky Derbies in 21 tries, but when he first started riding he was as rough as they come. Said he: "I came into racing setting traps, grabbing saddle cloths, and leg locking." One of the stewards of the time said he was "the roughest kid with whom I ever had to deal."

But Arcaro was given a wake-up call in the early '40s in the form of a one-year suspension from riding, and he became "Mr. Clean," so to speak.

The jockey whom Michael Matz wanted to ride Barbaro was a 38-year-old Peruvian-born jockey, Edgar Prado. His record is astonishing, one for the ages.

In 2004, he became only the 19th jockey in thoroughbred racing history—that's more than 130 years—to win over 5,000 races. Other racing accomplishments include victories in the 2002 and 2004 Belmont Stakes, in each case aboard a long shot and depriving a favorite of the Triple Crown. In 2002, Prado won the Belmont Stakes aboard "Sarava," who was the longest shot to ever win the Belmont Stakes at odds of 70.25–to–1. In 2004, Prado rode "Birdstone" to victory in the Belmont, denying heavy favorite Smarty Jones the Triple Crown. Prado and Birdstone then went on to win the prestigious Travers Stakes at the Saratoga Race Course in Saratoga Springs, New York, in August 2004. In 2000 and 2006, he won Breeder's Cup races.

Prado possesses all the characteristics great jockeys have: fearlessness, high intelligence, an ability to recognize race opportunities and make quick opportunistic decisions. And he is a passionate, loving man who connects with his horses. Why is connecting crucial? The horse can sense this love and gives back love to the jockey, which takes the form of doing what the jockey wants him to do. So many times one hears statements from great jockeys like "I asked him to run, and he started running with all his heart and soul."

Prado is also said to be a tempestuous—though not a rough—rider, and the jocks' room has served as a venue for battles with other jockeys not fought on the track, though certainly Prado is not

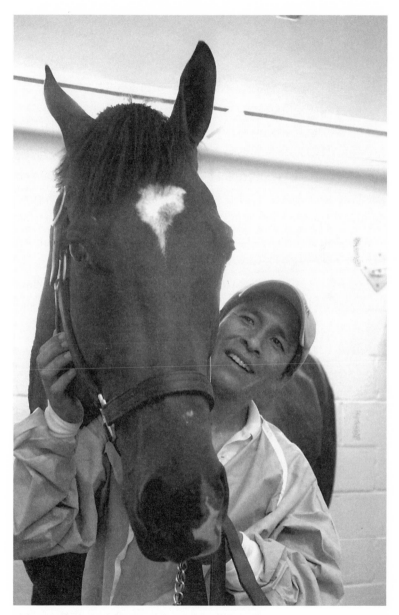

If love is the most important thing between a jockey and a horse, the great Prado and Barbaro have that.

alone. Horse racing is a highly volatile sport, and the men in it are hardly shrinking violets.

Prado was such a desirable jockey that his manager, Bob Frieze, said, "It's up to us who he wants to ride." Hence, Frieze said it was Prado who chose to ride Barbaro over a number of other mounts available.

Of course, jockeys have to be careful what horse they choose. Race history is littered with broken dreams of jockeys who rode the wrong horse, or dreams fulfilled when they accidentally rode the right one. For example, Eddie Arcaro didn't want to ride his first Derby winner, "Lawrin," and Earl Sande tried to move heaven and earth to ride "Quatrain" in the 1925 Derby but ended up riding "Flying Ebony" by default—and won.

Sometimes, who gets to ride what mount boils down to which one's available—it's that simple. And many times, the one the jockey selects is not the first choice of the owners or trainer. On April 17, 1999, following a win aboard "Key To Success,"—who was trained by D. Wayne Lukas—Chris Antley, who had almost killed himself with drugs but had fought back, was in the Winner's Circle at Santa Anita. At this time, Lukas approached him and told him that he wanted him and, if he was interested, to take a look the next day at a colt named "Charismatic," who had trained extra hard and who was running in the Coolmore Stakes in Lexington, Kentucky, the next day. What Antley didn't know was that not only Jerry Bailey but three other top riders—Chris McCarron, Lafitte Pincay, and Mike Smith—had already been asked by Lukas to ride Charismatic but had turned Lukas down. Antley observed Charismatic in the Coolmore Stakes, liked him, and went on to ride the horse and won both the Derby and the Preakness, and Charismatic was voted "Horse of the Year."

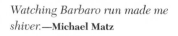

Watching Barbaro run made me shiver.—**Michael Matz**

Off to the Races!

6

As Barbaro grew, the Jacksons' hopes continued to grow with him. They became more confident that this was a very special horse, the champion they had longed for.

Michael Matz, of course, continued to think Barbaro was special too, and he was pointing him toward the Derby—and beyond. But here again: Just how good was he? And, as mentioned earlier, could he be competitive in races? Appearing good off the track is one thing, but there was nothing like seeing what a young colt could do in races against other colts. Thundering along on a training track is not the same thing as thundering along in a pack of horses among little men who scream nasty things about your mother and flail whips, a nerve-racking environment for horse and man.

Since he was pointing to the derby, the question for Matz then became which prep races he should run in. The key was entering races that Barbaro could handle at his particular age and that he had a chance to win. A horse has many traits and characteristics in his athleticism, just like a human being. As mentioned earlier, he may prefer a sprint to long distance, turf to dirt, different track conditions, etc. . . . the trainer can tell which he excels at by watching him and timing him. So, as the various prep races have different characteristics, it is possible to choose depending on what running conditions a horse favors. Matz did so by selecting a one-mile race. But that was not the only reason. He also explained that "one of the reasons we designed this plan for Barbaro was because he started so late in the season. He was an April 29 foal. We wanted to put him in races that would not be too much. His first race was in October and we spaced his races [leading to the Derby] at that point, and it just happened that his first race was on the grass. Then he ran the Laurel Futurity and the Tropical Park Derby. He always trained to suit his schedule." The key, of course, being to keep Barbaro, as Matz said, "fresh."

Barbaro's first race was October 4, 2005, the Maiden Special Weight, one mile in Delaware Park in Wilmington. In it he "broke his maiden" (won his first race) and definitively proved that racing on turf (his sire, Dynaformer, and dam, La Ville Rouge, had performed well on turf) was no problem. For this race, Jose Caballaro was his jockey. (Edgar Prado was in New York because, as his agent Bob Frieze explained, "he had other racing commitments.")

Barbaro's next race—also with Caballaro aboard—was a clear indication that Matz was following his core philosophy: Barbaro was entered in the Laurel Futurity on November 19, 2005, at Laurel, Maryland. This was six and a half weeks after his maiden race and 1⅟₁₆ mile longer than his first race. He covered this distance in 1:40.17, a lopsided victory. After the race, Matz said, "We thought he was a good horse from day one. He's living up to that expectation. This horse makes me shiver when I see him work on the dirt. He really does have a lot of talent."

Caballaro was also very impressed with Barbaro. He said:

"I was very confident with the horse. I've ridden him before. The horse was a little nervous behind the gate but broke well, and I was able to get him into a good spot. I didn't want to get in any trouble because I knew I had a good horse. You will be hearing a lot about this horse."

Six weeks later, Edgar Prado piloted Barbaro in the Tropical Park Derby, also on turf, held in Miami Gardens, Florida. The race was ⅟₁₆ mile longer than the Laurel Futurity, being 1⅛ mile long, ⅛ mile longer than his first race.

About five weeks later—still getting plenty of rest between starts—Matz entered Barbaro on a dirt-track race for the first time, at the Holy Bull Stakes in Hallandale Beach, Florida. It was a sloppy track, and he won.

Matz skipped most of the usual Derby prep races, even though they could be very revealing about a colt's chances in the Derby.

Barbaro winning the Laurel Futurity. Better things were to come!

The most popular final prep race for the Derby is the Blue Grass Stakes. Seventy eventual Derby winners ran their final prep race in the Blue Grass, the last being "Thunder Gulch" in 1995. Eleven eventual winners' last prep was in another popular race, the Wood Memorial, this with Funny Cide in 2003. The third most popular final prep race statistically is the Derby Trial. However, the last winner to come out of it was "Tim Tam" in 1958. The Derby Trial is no longer considered a viable prep race as it is a week prior to the Derby. This gives an indication of how prepping a horse for the Kentucky Derby is changing. The Santa Anita Derby has produced six Kentucky Derby winners.

The reason Barbaro missed those was because of their dates. They would have put him in races that were too close together. But he did not miss the Florida Derby. It was clearly the biggest race of Barbaro's young life. It's had quite a history. As Australian trainer Dan Blacker points out: "Derby winners Monarchos, Thunder Gulch, Unbridled, Swale, Spectacular Bid, Forward Pass, Northern Dancer, Carry Back, Tim Tam, and Needles all had victories in the Florida Derby prior to winning the Kentucky Derby." However, as detailed below, Needles in 1956 was the only horse out of these to go straight to the Derby without a further run like Thunder Gulch, Unbridled, Spectacular Bid, Forward Pass, and Northern Dancer, who all ran in the Blue Grass between the Florida and Kentucky Derby. Monarchos and Carry Back ran in the Wood, Swale ran in the Lexington, and Tim Tam ran in the Derby Trial. In looking at these statistics, bear in mind that two years ago, the Florida Derby moved from mid-March to early April. This would have allowed all these horses an extra week to get a run-in. Though Matz's focus was on Barbaro's training, it was not as if he and the Jacksons didn't notice that the prize money in the Florida Derby was one million dollars.

The race is 1⅛ mile long, and on this day it wasn't a walk in the park. Edgar Prado immediately put Barbaro, who was favored, in a perfect striking position, despite his breaking from post 10 in the field of 11 three-year-olds. Barbaro stalked the pace of "Sharp Humor" before challenging for command near the quarter pole and gaining a short advantage entering the stretch. Sharp Humor fought back from the inside before he finally lost in the last few yards by a half a length.

Barbaro had now won five races in a row. His next stop was Churchill Downs on the first Saturday in May 2006 . . . and maybe a couple of races after that he would be going after something called the Triple Crown.

But Matz's route to the big race was not without the criticism mentioned earlier when he first started to race train Barbaro. It was the old refrain: He had not raced or worked out Barbaro enough or entered him in enough races, but as the Derby approached, the criticism became more strident, perhaps in part because the media love controversy. Barbaro was compared to other horses who raced, and even worked out, much more frequently. What stood out about Barbaro's workouts, the media said, was the lack of them. Barbaro galloped only twice between the Florida Derby and Kentucky Derby. In addition, the workouts were over the relatively short distances of $\frac{4}{8}$ and $\frac{5}{8}$ mile. Compared to that, the 2005 Kentucky Derby winner, Giacomo, breezed four times over the same period of time and at distances of $\frac{6}{8}$ and $\frac{7}{8}$ mile and also raced in the Santa Anita Derby. The 2004 winner, Smarty Jones, breezed twice over $\frac{5}{8}$ mile, his final breeze in 58 flat, and ran in the Arkansas Derby. What's more, the last race Barbaro would be in was the Florida Derby on April 1, and therefore about five weeks before the Derby. Bottom line: He would not be in tip-top condition.

Answering the criticism, Matz, annoyed, said, "We know the dates of the Triple Crown. We didn't just make a decision by the seat of our pants. We knew what the dates of all the other prep races were. We could have gone into the Fountain of Youth [March 4 at Gulf Stream Park], but I wanted a fresh horse." It's a wonder he didn't say: "As I told you before!"

And he also said later, "I don't think Barbaro's preparation was different from traditional Derby preparation, whatever that may be. The horse will tell you what prep races to run in, and then you prepare the horse for those races as best you can. It was a preparation that suited the horse, and that's the most important thing. Barbaro had a five-week layoff between his final prep race and the Derby, as I believed that it would get the best run out of him in the Derby. Don't forget, he's a big horse."

As part of his explanation—or defense, if you will—of the importance of making sure a horse is properly rested between races, Matz cited the experience of Needles, the winner of the 1956 Kentucky Derby and the first Florida-bred colt ever to do so. He had a name that was, unfortunately, based on the many treatments that vets had given him to cure a wide variety of ailments he suffered as a foal.

As it turned out, Needles, who was the son of "Ponder," the 1949 Derby winner, grew up to be strong and healthy—those needles worked—and he was fast, very fast. As a two-year-old, he won the Florida Derby as well as the Flamingo Stakes.

There was a major question about how he would perform at Churchill Downs. For one thing, he had not run in a major-stakes race for six weeks prior to the Derby, or even worked out.

There was also the question of his style of running. The bridle, as it were, doesn't fall far from the tree. Like his father, Ponder (his mother's glorious name was "Noodle Soup"), Needles loved to come from behind—way behind.

To complicate the life of the horse, trainer, jockey, and owners, Needles drew post position number one, right on the rail. This might be fine for most horses but not desirable for a stretch runner, who would have a more difficult time working his or her way into position to make that run. Hugh Fontaine, Needles's trainer, could only joke about it. "I love it," he said. "I might as well love it because it's the only one I'm going to get."

When the race started, people's concerns about Needles getting too far behind to win seemed to come true. He was an astonishing 27 lengths behind with three-quarters of the race gone. He then started to move more quickly, but as he turned into the top of the stretch, he was still 15 lengths behind.

Not to worry. Said his jockey, Dave Erb, "When I asked him for it, he just went 'boom.' We found an opening about the three-eighths pole, went outside first, and then in."

Threading his way in and around other horses, Needles eventually wore "Fabius" down and won. It hardly seemed that infrequent training or racing had hurt him.

There was another criticism leveled at Matz related to prep. To wit: Over the course of the last century, while it was true that thoroughbred trainers have run their horses less frequently to win a Derby, a horse must have race experience. So in theory there must be a limit as to how little a horse can be prepped. Matz's only answer could be that he was doing what he thought was the best preparation for Barbaro.

Certainly he wasn't doing what the trainer did to "Donau," the horse that won the 1910 Derby. As a three-year-old prior to the Derby, Donau went to the post *41 times* and managed to win 15 of those races. Despite all this wear and tear—it would be like a major-league pitcher pitching 50 games a year—Donau (it means "Danube" in German) was the favorite in the Derby. But this race was his most difficult of all, and one of his most thrilling, with him able to hang on by a nose. With that many races prior to the Derby, it's a miracle he could stand up!

There is an ironic sidelight to all the brouhaha about preparation that many people do not know. Namely, that on the morning of the Kentucky Derby, Matz sent Barbaro out onto the track with his usual rider, Peter Brette, on board, for a steady gallop to stretch his legs and warm him up, so he did not pull out of his stall stiff at race time. Rumor has it that another horse doing a timed workout galloped past, and because Barbaro was so competitive, he sped up (with the rider trying to stop him) and caught the other horse and ran with him for ⅜ of a mile. Did that affect his Derby performance? Obviously not.

It was a fantastic time for the Jacksons. Their horse was entered in the greatest race of all and had a chance to become a champion,

BARBARO RACE DATA

Date	Race	Track	Location	Distance	Surface	Condition	Finish
October 4, 2005	Maiden	Delaware Park	Wilmington, Delaware	1 mi.	Turf	Firm	1st
November 19, 2005	Laurel Futurity	Laurel Park	Laurel, Maryland	1 1/16 mi.	Turf	Firm	1st
January 1, 2006	Tropical Park Derby	Calder Race Course	Miami Gardens, Florida	1⅛ mi.	Turf	Firm	1st
February 4, 2006	Holy Bull Stakes	Gulfstream Park	Hallandale Beach, Florida	1⅛ mi.	Dirt	Sloppy	1st
April 1, 2006	Florida Derby	Gulfstream Park	Hallandale Beach, Florida	1⅛ mi.	Dirt	Fast	1st
May 6, 2006	Kentucky Derby	Churchill Downs	Louisville, Kentucky	1¼ mi.	Dirt	Fast	1st
May 20, 2006	Preakness Stakes	Pimlico Race Course	Baltimore, Maryland	1 3/16 mi.	Dirt	Fast	DNF,* injury

*Did not finish.

something they had yearned and longed for for 30 years. This could be their moment.

Incredibly, their trip to Churchill Downs would be their first time ever, no less entering a horse in the Derby. For sure, this was a trip they were going to remember.

It's going to be very exciting when all these horses meet. This is what racing's about. It's up in the air and nobody knows who's going to win.—**Michael Matz**

It was breathtaking to see that horse win the way he did. . . . He was hand-ridden to the wire. It was like he was asking Prado, "How fast do you want me to go?"
—**Bill Sanborn**

Two Minutes to Glory

7

*I*t was a fairly warm first Saturday of May 2006 at Churchill Downs. The track was fast, the stands packed with over 157,000 well-dressed people, some wearing insane hats and a number of them sipping or chugalugging mint juleps to calm themselves or just to enjoy the day. And Michael Matz had some special visitors. As detailed in chapter 4, in 1989, a plane he was on turned into a fireball and he saved the lives of three young children, Melissa Roth Radcliffe and Travis and Jody Roth, who were 14, 12, and 9 respectively, when the plane crashed. Today, they were among the fans at Churchill Downs, and guess who they were rooting for!

But the crowd had a collective goal. They were getting ready to explode, because the bugle had sounded and now it was "post time."

And who knew, as the horses were led, coaxed, and pushed into their starting gates, how many years the owners, jockeys, trainers, and grooms had spent dreaming about this moment, dreaming not just of being in the race but of winning it? Today, those dreamers were represented by 20 horses—out of 440 nominations—and many had waited a long, long time, even decades, for this moment. And one of the couples, of course, was Gretchen and Roy Jackson, standing near the finish line, who had been involved with raising horses for 30 years and just wanted to breed a champion. This race could give them that—and then some.

Today, the Jacksons knew they had a terrific shot. They knew it, Michael Matz knew it, and their jockey, Edgar Prado, knew it, and so did every person who had ever been involved with their great horse, Barbaro. For one thing, as detailed earlier, Barbaro had a great pedigree on his side. His dad, Dynaformer, was an 11-year-old graded-stakes winner and a top sire in 2003, who had sired many other grade 1 greats such as Perfect Drift and Riskaverse (who stands today at Three Chimneys Farm for a mere $150,000 stud fee). And there was Barbaro's dam, La Ville Rouge, whom the Jacksons also own, a 10-year-old mare who won 6 out of 25 starts and is a daughter of Carson City, a sprinter who won 6 times in 15 lifetime starts.

But Barbaro was more than wonderfully pedigreed. He was *born a champion,* a big brawny horse with terrific speed and endurance.

The crowd seemed to know some things about the greatness of the horse too. They had made Barbaro the favorite, until at the last minute, someone had bet a large amount of money on "Sweetnorthernsaint" to make that runner the favorite.

But those were small odds in comparison to the odds of history. The numbers were against a favorite winning, and the numbers were astonishing. Out of 132 Derby winners, *only 47 favorites* had won the race . . . 85 had not, they'd lost, including some horses who experts said absolutely positively could not lose, such as Native Dancer, the overwhelming favorite in the 1953 Derby, who still lingers in memory. The winner of the 79th Kentucky Derby was Dark Star.

There was no question that Native Dancer, a light gray locomotive of a horse with the nickname "Gray Ghost"—probably because he would get ahead in a race and disappear from view—would win. It only remained for the race to occur to confirm it. As a two-year-old, he had won every race he had entered, and experts characterized him as not just one of the best horses of 1953 but one of the best racehorses ever.

And the world knew about him. In the early '50s, television was making its presence known in America's living rooms—and stations were more than happy to tell the world about this wondrous horse. He became famous.

But the problem with the Derby is that it's always unpredictable and no one told a brown colt named "Dark Star" that it was impossible to win.

When the race started, H. Moreno, Dark Star's jockey, immediately took the colt to the front. Native Dancer, with Eric Guerin aboard, was roughed up on the first turn by "Money Broker," which probably cost him dearly—some experts say he would have won if he hadn't been roughed up—and was eased back to secure racing room but, at the stretch, made a run for Dark Star and gained with every stride. Moreno, in a panic as Native Dancer closed, went to the whip, but it could not stop the inexorable drive of the Gray Ghost. He gained and gained and gained, and when they crossed the finish line, Native Dancer's nose was even with Dark Star's cheek, and he was gaining. The time was 2:02, and, of course, Dark Star had won.

Dark Star was a great horse, but many people do think he just got lucky that day when Native Dancer was roughed up in the beginning. From the Derby on, Native Dancer was in 22 races, and he won 21. In fact, the only time he ever lost was in the Kentucky Derby.

Whatever, all questions would be answered today.

At 6:15, the bell clanged and the gates opened. Immediately, the stomachs of those rooting for Barbaro went hollow as he stumbled but then regained his balance and Edgar Prado skillfully positioned him behind the pacesetting "Keyed Entry" and "Sinister Minster." All the horses were thundering along in a tight pack. In the stands, the fans were in full throat, but the knowledgeable ones knew that though the horses were moving front and back, this was not yet the race. The real race would come later.

They pounded on, then wheeled into the stretch, and now

the crowd got very loud because this was where the race really began. And "Heartbreak Lane" would be the specific place where all questions were answered. Would Matz's theories on how to train Barbaro hold up? Would the Jacksons' belief in the horse and Matz be proven right? Would Peter Brette, his exercise rider who had thought him great, be right? . . . Would, could Barbaro win . . . ?

And then boom! as if snapped out of the end of a long rubber band came Barbaro out of the pack at the top of that stretch, and the hysteria changed to a kind of muted reaction of amazement, and then the roar went up again, because Barbaro was abruptly, suddenly in the lead, pulling away with every stride. It appeared to be no contest.

One length, two lengths. Three lengths . . . and onward.

Prado, riding him by hand—not using a single whip stroke—looked back. There was no one to challenge him. All the other horses were racing for one thing: second money.

Down the stretch, Barbaro drove—the "wire," as jockeys say, coming to him and the announcer, semiberserk, yelling, "It's all Barbaro! It's all Barbaro!"

And it was, of course: He whacked across the wire 6½ lengths in the lead, achieving the second largest win since Assault had won by 8 lengths in 1946, achieving the 14th fastest time in the 132 year history of the race, and only a fifth of a second slower than "Affirmed," the last horse to win the Triple Crown 18 years earlier.

Those dreamers, the Jacksons, were speechless. And Edgar Prado displayed a smile that lit up his face like a neon sign, and so did Michael Matz.

Barbaro blasts to the wire in the Kentucky Derby.

Matz is not a man who is burdened with an overbearing ego. He's a plain-talking, hardworking person who says what he thinks. When he was asked by reporters what he thought of Barbaro's victory, which was achieved—to look at it another way—after being raced only once in the previous 13 weeks, the question clearly implied that he might look at it as a victory over his critics. But Matz merely said: "It's a moot point" and "I am not going to say a word." He was unable to even describe the horse's performance. "What can I say? Everybody saw it, so they know what he did."

As for Barbaro, his win made him an automatic favorite for the upcoming Preakness, the second leg of the Triple Crown. Matz, questioned again about his training tactics and, more important, how the previous uncommon five-week layoff might now backfire, now that Barbaro would have to run three back-to-back races in

Winner's Circle!

five weeks, thought he would be up to the challenge. "I don't think it's going to be a problem, but we will have to wait and see," he said. "If we made a mistake, we'll know it in two weeks. But that was the plan all along."

Roy and Gretchen Jackson had their own way of reacting. They were still in shock but were also unable to put the race into words. "We're sort of speechless," Roy said. "Just getting here was special, and winning it, I really don't have words to describe it."

But everyone was glad for them. "It couldn't happen to nicer people," said someone.

However, bad things, as a book's title, *When Bad Things Happen to Good People*, once said, happen to good people. And something very, very bad was about to happen to the Jacksons and a lot of other people, and to a great horse.

Man, those roses smell good!

KENTUCKY DERBY WINNERS VERSUS FAVORITES

Perhaps you thought we were kidding when we said that only 47 of 132 favorites had won the Derby. Barbaro's win kept that number at 47. Below is the list.

No.	Year	Winner	Favorite	Winner Odds
1	1875	Aristides, ch. c.	Winner (Entry)	2–1
2	1876	Vagrant, br. g.	Winner	9–5
3	1877	Baden-Baden, ch. c.	Leonard (7–5)	8–1
4	1878	Day Star, ch. c.	Himyar (14)	3–1
5	1879	Lord Murphy, b. c.	Winner	11–10
6	1880	Fonso, ch. c.	Kimball (3–5)	7–1
7	1881	Hindoo, b. c.	Winner	1–3
8	1882	Apollo, ch. g.	Runnymede (15)	10–1
9	1883	Leonatus, b. c.	Winner	9–5

No.	Year	Winner	Favorite	Winner Odds
10	1884	Buchanan, ch. c.	Audrain (2–1)	3–1
11	1885	Joe Cotton, ch. c.	Winner	Even
12	1886	Ben Ali, br. c.	Winner	1.72–1
13	1887	Montrose, b. c.	Banburg (7–5)	10–1
14	1888	Macbeth II, br. g.	Gallifet/Alexandria (Even)	6–1
15	1889	Spokane, ch. c.	Proctor Knott (1-2)	6–1
16	1890	Riley, b. c.	Robespierre (Even)	4–1
17	1891	Kingman, b. c.	Winner	1–2
18	1892	Azra, b. c.	Winner	3–2
19	1893	Lookout, ch. c.	Winner (Entry)	7–10
20	1894	Chant, b. c.	Winner	1–2
21	1895	Halma, blk. c.	Winner	1–3
22	1896	Ben Brush, b. c.	Winner	1–2
23	1897	Typhoon II, ch. c	Ornament (Even)	3–1
24	1898	Plaudit, br. c.	Lieber Karl (1–3)	3–1
25	1899	Manuel, b. c.	Winner	11–20
26	1900	Lieut. Gibson, b. c.	Winner	7–10
27	1901	His Eminence, b. c.	Alard Scheck (7–10)	3–1
28	1902	Alan-a-Dale, ch. c.	Abe Frank (3–5)	3–2
29	1903	Judge Himes, ch. c.	Early (3–5)	10–1
30	1904	Elwood, b. c.	Proceeds (Even)	15–1
31	1905	Agile, b. c.	Winner	1–3
32	1906	Sir Huon, b. c.	Winner	11–10
33	1907	Pink Star, b. c.	Red Gauntlet (1.50–1)	15–1
34	1908	Stone Street, b. c.	Sir Cleges (1.74–1)	23.72–1
35	1909	Wintergreen, b. c.	Winner	1.96–1
36	1910	Donau, b. c.	Winner	1.65–1
37	1911	Meridian, b. c.	Governor Gray (Even)	2.90–1
38	1912	Worth, br. c.	Winner	.80–1
39	1913	Donerail, b. c.	Ten Point (1.20–1)	91.45–1

No.	Year	Winner	Favorite	Winner Odds
40	1914	Old Rosebud, b. g.	Winner	.85–1
41	1915	Regret, ch. f.	Winner	2.65–1
42	1916	George Smith, blk. c.	Thunderer/Dominant (1.05–1)	4.15–1
43	1917	*Omar Khayyam, ch. c.	Ticket (1.45–1)	12.80–1
44	1918	Exterminator, ch. g.	*War Cloud (1.45–1)	29.60–1
45	1919	Sir Barton, ch. c.	Sailor/Eternal (2.10–1)	2.60–1
46	1920	Paul Jones, br. g.	Upset/Damask/Wildair (1.65–1)	16.20–1
47	1921	Behave Yourself, br. c.	Prudery/Tryster (1.10–1)	8.65–1
48	1922	Morvich, br. c.	Winner	1.20–1
49	1923	Zev, br. c.	Enchantment/Rialto/Picketer/Cherry Pie (2.30–1)	19.20–1
50	1924	Black Gold, blk. c.	Winner	1.75–1
51	1925	Flying Ebony, blk. c.	Quatrain (1.95–1)	3.15–1
52	1926	Bubbling Over, ch. c.	Winner (Entry)	1.90–1
53	1927	Whiskery, br. c.	Winner (Entry)	2.40–1
54	1928	Reigh Count, ch. c.	Winner (Entry)	2.06–1
55	1929	Clyde Van Dusen, ch. g.	Blue Larkspur/Bay Beauty (1.71–1)	3–1
56	1930	Gallant Fox, b. c.	Winner	1.19–1
57	1931	Twenty Grand, b. c.	Winner (Entry)	.88–1
58	1932	Burgoo King, ch. c.	Tick On (1.84–1)	5.62–1
59	1933	Brokers Tip, br. c.	Ladysman/Pomponius (1.43–1)	8.93–1
60	1934	Cavalcade, br. c.	Winner (Entry)	1.50–1
61	1935	Omaha, ch. c.	Nellie Flag (3.80–1)	4–1
62	1936	Bold Venture, ch. c.	Brevity (.80–1)	20.50–1
63	1937	War Admiral, br. c.	Winner	1.60–1
64	1938	Lawrin, br. c.	Fighting Fox (1.40–1)	8.60–1
65	1939	Johnstown, b. c.	Winner	.60–1
66	1940	Gallahadion, b. c.	Bimelech (.40–1)	35.20–1
67	1941	Whirlaway, ch. c.	Winner	2.90–1
68	1942	Shut Out, ch. c.	Winner (Entry)	1.90–1

No.	Year	Winner	Favorite	Winner Odds
69	1943	Count Fleet, br. c.	Winner	.40–1
70	1944	Pensive, ch. c.	Stir Up (1.40–1)	7.10–1
71	1945	Hoop Jr., b. c.	Pot o' Luck (3.30–1)	3.70–1
72	1946	Assault, ch. c.	Lord Boswell/Knockdown/ Perfect Bahram (1.10–1)	8.20–1
73	1947	Jet Pilot, ch. c.	Phalanx (2–1)	5.40–1
74	1948	Citation, b. c.	Winner (Entry)	.40–1
75	1949	Ponder, dk. b. c.	Olympia (.80–1)	16–1
76	1950	Middleground, ch. c.	Your Host (1.60–1)	7.90–1
77	1951	Count Turf, b. c.	Battle Morn (2.80–1)	f-14.60–1
78	1952	Hill Gail, dk. b. c.	Winner	1.10–1
79	1953	Dark Star, br. c.	Native Dancer (.70–1)	24.90–1
80	1954	Determine, gr. c.	Correlation (3–1)	4.30–1
81	1955	Swaps, ch. c.	Nashua (1.30–1)	2.80–1
82	1956	Needles, b. c.	Winner	1.60–1
83	1957	Iron Liege, b. c.	Bold Ruler (1.20–1)	8.40–1
84	1958	Tim Tam, dk. b. c.	Jewel's Reward/Ebony Pearl (2–1)	2.10–1
85	1959	*Tomy Lee, b. c.	First Landing (3.60–1)	3.70–1
86	1960	Venetian Way, ch. c.	Tompion (1.10–1)	6.30–1
87	1961	Carry Back, br. c.	Winner	2.50–1
88	1962	Decidedly, gr. c.	Ridan (1.10–1)	8.70–1
89	1963	Chateaugay, ch. c.	Candy Spots (1.50–1)	9.40–1
90	1964	Northern Dancer, b. c.	Hill Rise (1.40–1)	3.40–1
91	1965	Lucky Debonair, b. c.	Bold Lad (2–1)	4.30–1
92	1966	Kauai King, dk. b./br. c.	Winner	2.40–1
93	1967	Proud Clarion, b. c.	Damascus (1.70–1)	30.10–1
94	1968	Forward Pass, b. c.	Winner	2.20–1
95	1969	Majestic Prince, ch. c.	Winner	1.40–1
96	1970	Dust Commander, ch. c.	My Dad George (2.80–1)	15.30–1
97	1971	Canonero II, b. c.	Unconscious (2.80–1)	f-8.70–1

No.	Year	Winner	Favorite	Winner Odds
98	1972	Riva Ridge, b. c.	Winner	1.50–1
99	1973	Secretariat, ch. c.	Winner (Entry)	1.50–1
100	1974	Cannonade, b. c.	Winner (Entry)	1.50–1
101	1975	Foolish Pleasure, b. c.	Winner	1.90–1
102	1976	Bold Forbes, dk. b./br. c.	Honest Pleasure (.40–1)	3–1
103	1977	Seattle Slew, dk. b./br. c.	Winner	.50–1
104	1978	Affirmed, ch. c.	Alydar (1.20–1)	1.80–1
105	1979	Spectacular Bid, gr. c.	Winner	.60–1
106	1980	Genuine Risk, ch. f.	Rockhill Native (2.10–l)	13.30–1
107	1981	Pleasant Colony, dk. b./br. c.	Proud Appeal/Golden Derby (2.30–1)	3.50–1
108	1982	Gato Del Sol, gr. c.	Air Forbes Won (2.70–1)	21.20–1
109	1983	Sunny's Halo, ch. c.	Marfa/Balboa Native/Total Departure (2.40–1)	2.50–1
110	1984	Swale, dk. b. or br. c.	Life's Magic/Althea (2.80–1)	3.40–1
111	1985	Spend a Buck, b. c.	Chief's Crown (l.20–1)	4.10–1
112	1986	Ferdinand, ch. c.	Snow Chief (2.10–1)	17.70–l
113	1987	Alysheba, b.c. Alydar	Demons Begone (2.20–1)	8.40–1
114	1988	Winning Colors, ro. f.	Private Terms (3.40–1)	3.40–1
115	1989	Sunday Silence, dk. b./br. c.	Easy Goer/Awe Inspiring (.80–1)	3.10–1
116	1990	Unbridled, b. c.	Mister Frisky (1.90–1)	10.80–1
117	1991	Strike the Gold, ch. c.	Hansel (.50–1)	4.80–1
118	1992	Lil E. Tee, b. c.	Arazi (.90–1)	16.80–1
119	1993	Sea Hero, b.c.	Prairie Bayou (4.40–1)	12.90–1
120	1994	Go for Gin, b.c.	Holy Bull (2.20–1)	9.10–1
121	1995	Thunder Gulch, ch. c.	TimberCountry/Serena's Song (3.40–1)	24.50–1
122	1996	Grindstone, dk. b. or br. c.	Unbridled's Song (3.50–1)	5.90–1
123	1997	Silver Charm, gr. c.	Captain Bodgit (3.10–1)	4–1
124	1998	Real Quiet, b. c.	Indian Charlie (2.70–1)	5.40–1

No.	Year	Winner	Favorite	Winner Odds
125	1999	Charismatic, ch. c.	General Challenge (Entry) (4.80–1)	31.30–1
126	2000	Fusaichi Pegasus, b. c.	Winner	2.30–1
127	2001	Monarchos, gr. c.	Point Given (2–1)	9–1
128	2002	War Emblem, dk. b. or br. c.	Harlan's Holiday (6–1)	20.50 – 1
129	2003	Funny Cide, ch. g.	Empire Maker (2.50–1)	12.80 – 1
130	2004	Smarty Jones, ch. c.	Smarty Jones (4.10–1)	4.10 – 1
131	2005	Giacomo, gr./ro. c.	Bellamy Road (2.60–1)	50.30–1
132	2006	Barbaro dk. b. or br. c.	Brother Derek (3–1)	6.10–1

° *Foreign bred*

The Chance
of a Lifetime

8

Following his victory in the Derby, which was so decisive, Barbaro winning the Triple Crown became a very real possibility. But no one who knew anything about thoroughbred horse racing would count it as a sure thing. Far from it. The Triple Crown had a long and storied history—and was a crown that few people got to wear.

The title "Triple Crown" was created in the course of his writing by Charlie

Michael Matz, his wife, D-D, and the Jacksons at the Preakness. Happiness soon turned to tragedy.

Hatton, a writer for the *Daily Racing Form.* He came up with the phrase in writing about "Gallant Fox's" three victories in 1930. The Triple Crown had been the equine version of the pot of gold, not only making the horse's owner a lot of money but also collecting a king's ransom in prestige. Very few horses had been able to achieve it. Since the Derby was first held in 1875, there have only been 11 Triple Crown winners, or a little over 8 percent of the horses who've run in it. Forty-eight horses have won two of the three races.

Three Triple Crown champions were produced in the 1930s— Gallant Fox (1930), Omaha (1935), and War Admiral (1937). Gallant Fox sired Omaha, the 1935 winner, and is the only Triple Crown champion to sire another Triple Crown victor.

Four Triple Crown champions were crowned during the '40s,

beginning with Whirlaway in 1941. He was followed by Count Fleet (1943), Assault (1946), and Citation (1948).

Twenty-five years elapsed between Citation and Secretariat, who in 1973 accomplished the feat, smashing records in the Derby and Belmont en route to the prestigious award. In the years leading up to Secretariat's Triple Crown triumph, many doubted if there would be another Triple Crown winner. The Triple Crown had become more difficult to attain, with racing increased across the country and a larger number of foals produced yearly, producing more competition.

In 1977, Seattle Slew became the first unbeaten colt to sweep the Triple Crown, compiling nine consecutive victories, including the three jewels of the Triple Crown. Affirmed captured the coveted series a year later to become the 11th Triple Crown champion. His accomplishment marked the first time the Triple Crown has had winners in successive years. The death of Seattle Slew (May 7, 2002) marked the first time in history that there was no living Triple Crown champion to rule thoroughbred racing.

Why is it so difficult to become a Triple Crown champion? It not only tests a thoroughbred's speed but also his endurance, because the races are run so close together. It consists, of course, of three races: the Kentucky Derby, which is run on the first Saturday in May and is a mile and quarter long, followed two weeks later by the Preakness run on the Pimlico Race Course in Maryland, and is a mile and one sixteenth long, and, three weeks later, by the longest of all, the Belmont Stakes, which is a mile and a half long.

The plain fact is that three years old is a young age for a horse to take on such major physical hurdles. Its bones are young, and many times its body can't stand the exertion. Sometimes the effort it expends will be so strenuous that it will bleed from the lungs. Indeed, this is why so-called bleeders—horses with a propensity to bleed—are given a drug called Lasix to prevent it. But it often still occurs, and when a horse starts bleeding from the nostrils, it is quite a disruptive experience.

The thing that had people thinking that Barbaro would take the crown was the quality of his victory in the Derby. He had not only won the race but obliterated the competition in very good time. Plus, he is a big, powerful horse who had a great trainer and jockey. What could stop him? But one old-time trainer—50 years in racing—Lucas James, commented, "I've heard that song before."

There was no question that the races being bunched up for Barbaro were opposed by Michael Matz's basic racing philosophy of not working horses. The Triple Crown imposed a schedule that Barbaro had never yet to contend with. Barbaro went into the Kentucky Derby undefeated, having raced just five times in his career. Only one other horse in the field of 20 had run less—his stable mate, "Showing Up." Matz admits that the effects of racing his horse on such a widely spaced schedule and then suddenly running him two weeks apart in hugely demanding races such as the Derby and Preakness are unknown. Speaking of Barbaro, Matz said, "I'm sure it took something out of him, but what Kentucky Derby doesn't take something out of them? He's eating good; his blood was good. He's going to the track fine. I don't think anyone knows how a horse is affected [running] within just two weeks.

"I didn't want to get a horse that maybe peaked at the Kentucky Derby and doesn't have anything left. Sometimes, a lot of these horses are raced or burnt out by the time they get to Kentucky. I didn't want to use him up."

Barbaro did not get a timed workout between the Kentucky Derby and the Preakness. Matz did nothing more than jog Barbaro when he returned from Churchill Downs, but the horse stepped up the first week back. On Tuesday morning, Barbaro galloped 1½ miles under exercise rider Peter Brette for a large group watching from the Fair Hill track's clock tower.

Training Barbaro at Fair Hill was very important to Matz. One of the things he wanted to do after Barbaro's Derby Triumph was to make sure the horse had peace and quiet, that he was not only physically but also mentally rested. But that's hard with a superstar because of the attention of the fans, and if Matz didn't know that, then he knew it when he vanned Barbaro from the Derby to his Fair Hill Training Center in Maryland. When he got there, he found a group of Amish people in the barn milling around to get a glimpse of the great horse. Shortly thereafter, a woman came with her two young daughters to take a gander, and, Matz said, he also saw a guy pushing another guy in a wheelchair up to the barn, and Matz said, "What are you doing?" And the man answered, "I'm here to see Barbaro."

But Fair Hill was still Fair Hill—quiet and beautiful, 350 acres of Maryland countryside that someone said "rolls like a painting in a child's picture book." Beautiful grazing horses, surrounded by mesh paddocks, dot the landscape, and here and there are crisply bright painted barns. Fair Hill is quite different from the relatively cacophonous and busy environment of Pimlico Race Course, a complex surrounded by asphalt, noise, and voluminous traffic.

Knowing the ambience—or absence of ambience—at Pimlico, Matz was determined to keep Barbaro away from it for as long as he could. Indeed, if he could have, he would have vanned him to

Pimlico the morning of the race, Saturday, if it had not promised to be so crowded that he might have difficulty getting there. As it happened, most of the horses in the Preakness arrived at Pimlico on Tuesday, May 16, while Matz arrived with Barbaro on Friday morning.

During this period, Matz himself was quite intense, absolutely focused on Barbaro and how best to get him ready for the Preakness. "That's Michael," one of his colleagues said. "You can tell him stuff, and he doesn't take it in. I think if it's about the horse—and he's so focused on the horse—and you're talking about the horse, he's listening. I don't know anybody who's more acutely aware of what's going on with a horse than Michael. His antennae are finely, finely tuned." The nearly overwhelming volume of responsibility leaves Matz looking focused at one moment, distracted the next; tense and patient, then enjoying a belly laugh.

In addition to Barbaro, Matz was also responsible for getting about 50 other horses that spent the winter in Florida used to feeling at home at Fair Hill Training Center and handling a stable of 20 more runners at Delaware Park. And then there was, of course, dealing with the racing-writer fraternity, for whom Barbaro had suddenly made great copy. Matz continued to train Barbaro with an accent on not overtraining him and leaving his race, or races, as it were, in the paddock.

On one of the days, it rained, and Matz didn't want to run Barbaro until the rain stopped. In the late morning, he asked Sally Goswell, general manager at Fair Hill, if the wood-chip training track could be leveled out with a screen roller, and she obliged. "That wasn't a problem," Goswell said. "Michael has always been great to deal with. I don't necessarily see him every day, but he just seems great to me. The guys who do the track maintenance were up here this morning, and he was talking to them. He seems to have time for everybody, but I would have to think, seeing what I've seen, that training Barbaro is a full-time job. People need to realize this isn't the only horse he is training."

But in truth, Barbaro was the only horse in training. None of the others had the chance of a lifetime, as he did.

The Preakness Stakes, which Barbaro was going to try to conquer, is the shortest of the Triple Crown races at 1¹⁄₁₆ mile. Colts (horses under five years old) and geldings carry 126 pounds (57 kg); fillies, 121 lb (55 kg). The Preakness Stakes has been termed "the Run for the Black-Eyed Susans" because a horseshoe of black-eyed Susans, *Rudbeckia hirta,* the state flower of Maryland, is traditionally placed around the winner's neck. It almost always attracts the Kentucky Derby winner, some of the other horses that ran in the Derby, and often a few horses that did not start in the Derby.

Pimlico has been around for a long time. Two years before the Kentucky Derby was run for the first time, Pimlico introduced its new stakes race for three-year-olds, the Preakness, during its first-ever spring race meet in 1873. Governor Oden Bowie had named the then 1½-mile (2.41-km) race in honor of Dinner Party Stakes winner "Preakness," from the Preakness Stables in Wayne, New Jersey.

Just after the horses for the Preakness are called to the post, the audience is invited to sing "Maryland, My Maryland," the official song of the state. Traditionally, the United States Naval Academy Glee Club assembles in the Pimlico infield to lead the song. This tradition mirrors the singing of "My Old Kentucky Home" at the post parade for the Kentucky Derby. And as soon as the Preakness winner has been declared officially, a painter climbs a ladder to the top of a replica of the old clubhouse cupola and the colors of the victorious owner's silks are applied; a horseshoe of black-eyed Susans is also placed around the winning horse's neck at this time, and a replica of the Woodlawn vase is given to the winning horse's owner. Or, the Jacksons were hoping . . . owners.

Disaster

9

A number of people viewing the Preakness noticed it.

The Preakness was almost starting. People were watching Barbaro approach the gate from behind it, maybe 75 yards away, when suddenly his jockey, Edgar Prado, turned and looked down at the horse's right rear leg. Then the horse took another step or two, and Prado looked again. The silent question occurred. *Was he hurt?*

But Barbaro seemed to be all right, because Prado then proceeded to the gate and they loaded Barbaro in along with the other horses.

Then came another upsetting incident. The camera had a full shot of the loaded horses facing it, and quickly and shockingly one of the horses slammed through the electric gate, which, like other gates, are held closed magnetically with an electrical charge. It was Barbaro, and again there was concern that he was hurt.

But he wasn't. He was led back into the starting gate by outriders—they're there to handle just such false starts, and some people watching breathed a sigh of relief. Then the bell went off, gates opened—and the horses broke out, starting normally.

And then came the real disaster.

Millions of viewers watched the horses break out, and it's a safe bet that many of them were watching the jockey with the green-and-white silks on, Edgar Prado, and Barbaro to see if there was any further disruption. Also, a ton of money had been bet on him and he was a two-to-one favorite. It was no secret, of course, that many people felt he had the potential to become the first Triple Crown winner in 28 years.

Thundering toward the camera, the horses had not even started to drift toward the first turn when it happened: The screaming crowd acted, collectively, as if it had been punched in the stomach, as they saw Barbaro, a couple of hundred yards from the starting gate, being pulled up by Edgar Prado, who immediately jumped off and held the horse by the reins.

Then came the heartbreaking sight of big, beautiful Barbaro—somehow like a helpless child—standing on three legs, holding his right hind foot off the ground. He was no longer putting pressure

Edgar Prado tries to support an injured Barbaro. His right hind leg was fractured.

on the leg, so it looked like to some people as if he might be okay. But he wasn't. Barbaro's connections knew how serious it was. They came running.

Michael Matz ran from the clubhouse to the racetrack with Gretchen and Roy Jackson behind him. Peter Brette, Barbaro's exercise rider, raced from the paddock to Edgar Prado, who was bent over at the waist in agony. They hugged and cried. Yes, they knew. And so did D-D, Matz's wife, who, as mentioned earlier, was a very experienced horsewoman: She was engulfed in grief.

At one point the horror multiplied. Workers brought out a green screen to place between Barbaro and the world. Some people knew what it was for—to possibly euthanize the horse and keep the horrific act from everyone's sight.

People started to cry and scream. "No! No! No!" one distraught woman by the rail screamed. "Do not put that horse down! Don't you dare put him down! I'll buy him for a dollar!"

People in the crowd screamed also: "No! No!"

"Take him home!!"

"Get him on the van!"

Dr. Lawrence Bramlage immediately came down from his position in the jockey quarters and behind the screen and examined Barbaro, who was still not bearing any weight on his "right hind," as vets say. One of the things the doctor was looking for was to see if the skin was broken. "If it was," he said, "it could introduce infection." And though he didn't state it overtly, his presence would be needed in the decision to euthanize Barbaro.

But the skin was not broken.

A Kimzey splint with a cup for this foot and straps that go up to the hock was put on his leg to stabilize it, and, following standard procedure, a white horse ambulance came onto the track. The back was lowered, and, Dr. Bramlage said, "Barbaro hopped on using three legs. It wasn't difficult for him, because he is a great athlete."

Fifteen or 20 years ago, a team would have come out, and Barbaro would likely have been euthanized. But not today. It was quickly determined that the injury was, as Dr. Bramlage said, "on the cutting edge of what we can handle."

And Barbaro helped himself. "Big, tough horses," said the doctor, "are surprisingly good patients. And they do a lot of the right things for themselves when they're injured. They're not hard to manage. Frisky young horses are usually a problem."

Dr. Bramlage got on the ambulance with the horse, and they

went back to his stall, where Dr. Nick Mettinis, a private vet, waited. Said Mettinis: "He came off the van with the splint that was applied on the racetrack. He was sedated and backed off the van without putting any weight on the leg. After we X-rayed the leg and found what it consisted of, we put a very large padded bandage on him and the entire time the bandage went on he never moved a muscle. That's going to be critical in his recuperation. His temperament is going to help him in his recuperative state."

Another vet, Dr. Dan Dreyfuss, Barbaro's attending physician, took radiographs. Then a new, better cast was put on by Drs. Dreyfuss and Meittinis. Throughout this entire period Barbaro was being a very good patient.

Within half an hour, a decision had been made as to where to send Barbaro for further help: the New Bolton Center, a veterinarian hospital attached to the University of Pennsylvania, in Kennett Square.

Michael Matz lived just down the road from the facility, and he had brought other horses there. In fact, it was one of the best large-animal hospitals in the country, and, as it happened, it also had one of the best veterinary surgeons in Dr. Dean Richardson, who was also good friends with Matz. It was assumed that Richardson would do the surgery, and toward that end Dr. Dreyfuss had sent him the radiographs by e-mail to a hospital in West Palm Beach, Florida, where Dr. Richardson performed surgery.

Whoever was going to be performing the surgery on Barbaro, it was quickly determined that it would not be done that night. Barbaro was still filled with high-voltage energy that was ready to be expelled during the race, and then there was the stress of the injury. "To put him through the stress of an operation where he would wake up from anesthesia not knowing where he was," Dr. Bramlage said, "could make him panic and have a greater chance of inflicting additional injuries upon himself. Tomorrow was soon enough. If you have your choice, you would like to settle the horse down, get him used to the fact that he has a fracture. He becomes a much better patient for anesthesia and recovery from anesthesia, which as everyone knows is a major obstacle for a horse of 1,200 pounds."

After the X rays, which vets call "radiographs," were taken, Barbaro was loaded into the ambulance, which was fine for highway driving and is equipped to make it safe for the horse. The ambulance had an inside movable wall that could be used to create a narrow space that restricted Barbaro's movement. But Dr. Dreyfuss, who would be traveling with him in the ambulance, did not feel he had to restrict Barbaro's space. By moving the wall close to him, Barbaro was being a perfectly good patient.

At 7:22 P.M., a caravan that included a state police escort and others, including the Matzes and the Jacksons, started out for the New Bolton Center. The trip took a little over an hour, the caravan arriving in the darkness. Already there were fans, well-wishers, and the hospital staff. The world waited and held its breath.

I hope there's some knowledge that owners and trainers and jockeys care. It's not about money, it's not about limelight, it's more about the horse and the beauty of it and the integrity of it on a lot of levels.
—**Gretchen Jackson**

Not letting a mockingbird die is what makes us human.—**Catherine Philbin**

America Puts Its Arms Around Barbaro

10

*E*very now and then the American public opens its hearts to an athlete, human or otherwise, and puts its collective arms around him or her and forms a special, complicated bond. In the world of horse racing, for example, and even though his career spanned only three years in the 1920s, Man o' War was perhaps the greatest racehorse who ever lived and was adored by people. By the time he died on November 1, 1947, after a highly successful 20-year stud career, over a million fans had visited him at Faraway Farm. And over 2,000 people turned out for his funeral—which was broadcast on radio nationwide. In 1973, there was Secretariat, who broke the two-minute barrier in the Derby and never went a day during the 19 years of his existence without fans visiting him. There was "Black Gold," the legendary 1924 Derby winner who ultimately died on a racetrack and was christened "the People's Horse," and "Regret," who in 1915 became the first filly ever to win the Derby, and Funny Cide, owned by a group of ordinary Joes, who became part of a miracle in 2003 when he won the Kentucky Derby.

And now one can add another name to the list: Barbaro. America's love for this horse became apparent after the Derby and before the Preakness, and then after he hurt himself. Why? Perhaps, as Gretchen Jackson said, it's "about integrity on many different levels." Perhaps, also, because he was so obviously a great horse, a beautiful horse, and a stunning example of what human beings can breed. Perhaps it is also because America felt that for the first time in almost 30 years, it had a genuine candidate to win the Triple Crown, and partly because his disposition was known. Barbaro was no psychotic ear-biting Mike Tyson, or a brooding Sonny Liston, or a bigoted Ty Cobb, or a pissed-off Jimmy Brown, or an Omaha, the 1935 Triple Crown winner who liked to bite other horses. Barbaro was a great athlete who also happened to have a wonderful personality. "A horse," one of his trainers had once said, "who was everything you could ever want."

And then the mind-numbing tragedy at the Preakness occurred, and the silent admiration and affection for this horse burst forth,

Pimlico. Within hours an unparalleled outpouring of love started for Barbaro. Tens of thousands of fans signed get-well banners and cards. Ultimately, his Web site had over 2 million visits.

Niagara Falls–like, found its voice, and everywhere you looked you could see it, feel it, hear it. This was a horse that people from all walks of life wanted—needed—to live. Actually or instinctively, they knew the big truth: You can't kill a mockingbird, or let it die.

In the Preakness postrace news conference, for example, attended by jockeys, trainers, and owners, concern for the horse came through. Said Javier Castellano, the jockey who piloted "Bernadini" to victory, "I didn't see the horse coming out. I didn't see what happened. Afterward, I realized that it was Barbaro—he was right in the middle of the track. I saw the jockey, oh, my God. Really, really sad." Said Nick Zito, the hard-boiled Hall of Fame trainer of the third-place finisher, "Hemingway II": "The whole story is this. Let's just hope Barbaro lives." Jeremy Rose, jockey of "Hemingway's Key, 3rd," said: "My horse ran a great race. It set up all right for him. We got thrown around most of the way. It is hard to celebrate with what happened to Barbaro when he gets vanned off and it does not look good." Said the trainer, Michael Trobotta, of Sweetnorthernsaint, who was 2nd: "This is terrible."

Fans in droves expressed their concern. Right away at Pimlico, a three-foot-by-ten-foot banner, which featured the green, white, and blue silks of Barbaro's owners, was made, reading: "All the best, Barbaro . . . With love from your friends at Pimlico." And then fans started to sign it in droves. It was hung in the grandstand and ultimately would make it into the stall in the intensive care unit (ICU) in the New Bolton Center, where Barbaro would be cared for.

A couple of days after the accident, Roy Jackson said he spoke with a reporter from *The New York Times,* and "he said their story in Sunday and Monday was read more—or twice as much as—any story they covered." He had no idea why, but Barbaro captured the "popularity or whatever you want to say of the American people. I just think it's a wonderful thing."

But fan support hardly stopped there. Once it was learned where Barbaro was, the hospital was under a beautiful siege of letters, signed telegrams, packages of fruit, vegetables, gifts, money, and cards galore—in the thousands and, ultimately, the tens of thousands, and e-mails—over two million of them have been recorded on the Barbaro Web site. And the sentiments were as heartfelt as you can get.

"You are too beautiful to die."

"Don't worry, Barbaro, God will hold you in his arms."

"No one could beat you in the Derby, and nothing can beat you now."

"I love you, Barbaro. Each day when I wake up I say a prayer for you, and every
night before I go to bed I ask God to watch over you."

"Hey Big boy. How you doin? Don't be afraid. You're going to be fine."

"Believe in Barbaro."

Barbaro also had many visitors, and though no one was allowed in the ICU to see Barbaro, that didn't stop them from making their presence felt.

But through it all, of course, the burning, terrible question on people's minds was: Would he survive? A number of people took a route that many take these days when under great stress. Some actually consulted psychics, asking to consult, through them, loved ones who have passed or "crossed over" to help them with Barbaro's ordeal.

One person, Anne Lundy of Huntington Station, New York, reported seeing Barbaro in a psychic dream, in which the colors are more vivid than in a regular dream. Another way to tell it's psychic is that one simply senses it is. Lundy described her experience to one of the authors: "I was in a field, she said,

surrounded by a large fence and there were a lot of people—thousands—behind the fence and they were all staring at me and a lot of them were crying. It definitely was a psychic dream because everything was rich and colorful. The ground I was on was a chocolate brown and the people were dressed in incredibly colorful clothes and the sky when I looked up was a very rich blue.

I had no idea why they were crying, but as I looked at their faces I caught something out of the side of my eye. It was in the chocolate-covered dirt and *was silver and glistening brightly. At first I couldn't make out what it was, but when I approached it I saw that it was a horseshoe, but not an ordinary horseshoe. It looked like it was made of pure silver.*

I asked myself, I wonder where that came from, and as I looked again my eyes passed across the crowd and I could see their faces—they all had incredibly white teeth—and now they don't look sad. I wondered what was going on, and then I saw that a number of them were pointing behind me at something and in that instant I realized that the chocolate dirt area I was on was a track.

I turned and saw this beautiful bay horse, and then I saw a little white diamond-shaped mark on his forehead and I started to cry because I knew it was Barbaro, and I knew he would live. And he will.

Many of the communications and gifts were religious in nature. One of the gifts Barbaro received was a box of holy water from the River Jordan, sent by Sheikh Mohammed al Maktoum and his wife. Sheikh Mohammed owns Bernardini, who won victories in the Preakness, Jim Dandy, Travers, and Jockey Club Gold Cup before he retired in 2006.

Another gift, one that stands inside the lobby of the hospital, is a statue of St. Francis, the patron saint of animals.

Many people have also had masses said for Barbaro and sent him holy pictures, Mass cards, and more. And a lot of people went to Mass and other religious services to offer prayers to him. One young girl said, "I had stopped going to Mass until Barbaro was injured. But I didn't know where to turn to try to get help to save him, and the only person I could turn to was Jesus Christ. I now go to Mass twice a week—more if I can—and pray for him. And so far it's working."

And another person said he made a sort of pilgrimage to a park near Villa Avenue in the Bronx where for many years the Blessed Virgin Mary was said to have appeared. Though the shrine was no longer there, the man remembered where it was and said a few prayers there.

If there was ever any doubt about the love Roy and Gretchen Jackson had for Barbaro, the little matter—or not so little matter—of insurance should settle that. When Barbaro broke down, the couple was holding millions of dollars in insurance—an estimated $25 to $30 million—to cover any "catastrophic injury." All they had to do was put Barbaro down. They didn't. "There couldn't be enough money in the world to do that," Gretchen Jackson said. Indeed, there isn't even coverage for Barbaro's medical bills, which will be extensive.

On May 23, 2006, just three days after Barbaro was injured, the University of Pennsylvania made an announcement: "Love has also showed up in the form of money. An anonymous donor has given a very generous gift to launch the Barbaro Fund for the George D. Widener Hospital at New Bolton Center. Due to the overwhelming outpouring of support for Barbaro, the University of Pennsylvania's School of Veterinary Medicine has also established a Web site where people can send messages of support for Barbaro and where donors can offer their support for animals treated at New Bolton Center."

"It is wonderful that we can create something so very good out of Barbaro's tragedy and to help celebrate animal athletes," said Gretchen Jackson. "This fund in Barbaro's name will honor him and provide a lasting resource to help care for animals treated at the Widener Hospital."

Donations will go directly to a fund for the Widener Hospital and not be restricted to Barbaro's care. So far, $1.25 million has been donated.

Dan Blacker, an Australian trainer, who had witnessed what was going on from afar—in Australia—said, "While there was an out-pouring of love, there was something still percolating in the minds of people, including people who were focused on expressing their love and good wishes in any way they could. Namely, no one could definitively say what had caused the injury: What made it happen? A number of people looked hard at it and tried to explain it."

"I think it's good to set the record straight," said Dr. David Zipf, chief veterinarian for the Maryland Racing Commission and the vet who was responsible for the health of the horses at the starting gate. Zipf had been right there at the track, observing everything. "I was standing behind the gate when he broke through," Zipf said. "I followed him through the gate. As they turned him, I watched for a nosebleed, bruises, or a shoulder injury. I walked out about fifteen or twenty-five feet, about at the spot where the outriders caught him. Then I trailed him to see how he was moving. I could see no problems. If there had been, I would have called the stewards and asked for more time. But he looked perfect."

Jerry Bailey, an ex-jockey with decades of experience in racing as a jockey—in fact, another all-time all-starter, and now an ESPN commentator—didn't see an injury related to the false start. "He broke very well," Bailey said. "If he had injured his back leg before the break for the race, he probably would not have left the gate very well. It affects his pushing power. He would've broken slug-gishly."

Michael Matz, Edgar Prado, and Barbaro's surgeons do not believe the injury was due to the false start either. "Michael trained that horse to perfection," said one trainer. "Let's not overlook that. I've known Michael a long, long time, since I was a young kid. If there was any indication of a problem, that horse would never have left the stall."

A host of trainers and other officials said the same thing: The injury was not due to the false start. Nor did Barbaro have any preexisting injuries. Zipf examined him the morning of the Preakness. "I physically checked his legs in the morning," Zipf said. "I watched him being saddled, and I watched him walk after the false start. I was doing what I was supposed to be doing, and he looked perfect."

And more than just one set of official eyes were watching the horses before the start. Additionally, said John McDaniel, chairman of the Maryland Racing Commission, "There are about a dozen binoculars on them. The stewards, the vet, the starters. If a horse isn't physically well, there is a standard procedure. A call would be made."

Some people had suggested that Barbaro could have had the accident before he entered the starting gate. Dr. Bramlage did not think so. "No," Bramlage said, "it couldn't have happened earlier because he broke out of the gate and was going wherever his action began to—when Edgar felt something was wrong—so this happened sometime after he was going in the, what, the first furlong or so. Edgar Prado probably knew something was wrong when that first fracture happened, but the horse doesn't likely know that. They don't sense it even in the end. If Edgar had let him go, he probably would have tried to chase him around the field because it doesn't hurt initially with all that adrenaline rush, especially when you tear the covering of the bone, where the—where all nerve supply is. The horse feels relatively nothing until the inflammation sets in. Edgar was probably more aware that he was injured than the horse was.

"In my opinion," Bramlage continued, "this had nothing to do with him breaking through the gate as far as a cause and effect of the fracture in his leg. He wouldn't have been able to go around the gate, get back in, and break like he did."

All this expert opinion notwithstanding, two things happened as Barbaro paraded to the gate that are worth noting. For one thing, Barbaro bucked. Like others, Zipf saw Barbaro bucking and observed Prado looking back at Barbaro's hind leg.

"He looked right and left," Zipf said. "He felt the horse jump and was looking to see if he got scalped. That's what we call it when a horse sometimes overreaches with his hind legs and gets hooked by the front hooves. He looked and I looked, and there was nothing, no scratches."

The final conclusion of most of the people who tried to determine what caused the injury was just that it was a freak accident: Barbaro took a bad step on the track after the race started. Said Jerry Bailey: "When athletes of any kind perform at the highest level, they're susceptible to injury."

The Barbaro Fund
"Trustees of the University of Pennsylvania"
Office of Development and Alumni Relations
University of Pennsylvania
School of Veterinary Medicine
3800 Spruce Street
Philadelphia, PA 19104-6047

The Man Who Would Try to Save Barbaro

11

*B*ack in his college undergraduate days, Dean Richardson had no idea that he would become a vet, much less a veterinary surgeon. As an undergraduate at Dartmouth College in New Hampshire in the early '70s, he says, "I first wanted to be an actor. When I went to sign up for phys. ed.—there were PE requirements back then—there was a list of options, basketball, football, weight lifting, baseball, football, and some others, that I'd already done in high school. There was one thing on the list I hadn't done: horseback riding. This course was taught by Marilyn Blodgett on her farm out at Velvet Rocks. So I signed up."

"It wasn't really a farm," Blodgett says. Blodgett, who now lives in Hanover, New Hampshire, says that it was "just four acres one side of Truscott Road and four on the other."

Amazingly, Richardson had never ridden a horse when he signed up for the course.

"But," Blodgett said, "he loved it. He came to the farm every day. Within a week he was able to walk, trot, and canter the horse, and in no time I got him jumping. He was a well-balanced human being. Often all I told him was 'Keep your hands light!'"

And, Richardson said, he "fell in love with horses."

Richardson is a competitive kind of person, as most surgeons—animal or human—are. And he soon became a competitive rider. He also became a member of the Hanover Pony Club—"The best you can get," Blodgett says.

In his junior year, Richardson moved into the farmhouse on the property with Blodgett's son, Peter, another Dartmouth student, and two young ladies. They posted a sign on the barn: "There are no bad horses, only bad riders." "We took care of eighteen horses," Peter said, "Dean was funny, he was playful, and he loved to ride."

At one point, his love for horses transmuted into a desire to be an equine surgeon, to help horses in a kind of ultimate way. He applied to, and got accepted by, the Ohio State Veterinary School in 1974. He arrived at New Bolton in 1979.

Says Dr. Mitch Leitch, who was Richardson's supervisor back

then, "I knew the day I met him he would be the best intern I ever had. He was—he is—one of the smartest people I've ever known. He has a tremendous ability to recall and integrate information. I didn't know what kind of hands he had." Ultimately, she characterized them with a single word: "magical."

And Richardson, of course, was hardly adverse to expressing his opinion. Leitch said that she was glad she had six years of clinical experience because, she said, without it "I would have been intimidated. He is a powerful intellectual force."

Richardson is different from other surgeons, Leitch says, because he can see how everything goes together, but what sets him apart is that he sees possibilities that allow him a grasp of a "fourth dimension." Leitch said that he will work on cases that ordinarily would be unlikely to have successful outcomes.

At New Bolton Center, now the chief of surgery, Richardson is still an intimidating force, particularly among the interns. Every Thursday, when he is in town—and he is much in demand as a speaker because he has penned the definitive books on equine surgery—he meets with New Bolton interns and the students present their cases for critiquing. They fear his questions, because it is a no-holds-barred critique and he says what he thinks and is basically a perfectionist, with a warehouse full of clinical experience in his head.

And don't expect him to forget much. He remembers everything, even the names of horses and their owners who have come to the hospital. Understandably, some of the interns are glad when he's out of town, unavailable for the Q & A, which has come to be known as the "Grand Tour."

On the day that Barbaro broke down, Richardson was, as mentioned earlier, out of town. This time he was at a friend's hospital in Loxahatchee, Florida, in West Palm Beach performing various equine surgeries, such as a "sinus surgery that ran about two a half hours. Another which lasted four hours involved taking a bladder stone out of a show horse."

For much of the day, "he had blood all over him," said Dr. Byron Reid, a friend and vet in Loxahatchee, Florida, just outside West Palm Beach, "and we were doing it in flip-flops, so we hosed him off." But Richardson was not about to miss the Preakness. He was a thoroughbred racing fan and rider, particularly since Barbaro was to be in it and Richardson had, as also mentioned earlier, operated more than once on the horses of Michael Matz.

He stepped out of the operating room to watch the race on a six-inch television screen. Like millions of others, he watched as Barbaro false-started, then watched as the bell clanged and the gates opened and the cavalry charge commenced. Then suddenly, Edgar Prado, Barbaro's jockey, pulled the horse up. Instantly, Richardson knew what many people did not as Barbaro stood on three legs, his right rear hoof off the track. "My stomach started to churn," he said. "I knew it was a very bad injury."

His response was to do nothing. He knew that the people on site at the track had their work cut out for them, because he knew instantly—knowing Matz and the Jacksons—that Barbaro was not going to be euthanized. "There was just no way that was going to happen," he said. And no one was going to operate on Barbaro today. Sunday would be soon enough.

As he had expected, no one called him in the first few minutes. Then came the calls from the scene and the radiographs of

Barbaro's shattered leg. He soon learned what he had suspected: Matz and the Jacksons wanted him to try to save Barbaro's life.

He instantly said yes, but he knew also that he was going to be functioning inside the eye of a tornado of public and media interest, and that the horse on the operating table was worth millions of dollars. He had done important, high-stakes operations before. But that didn't matter. When the horse is on the operating table, he says, it's not Barbaro, it's "just a horse in trouble." And all Richardson focuses on is how to help the horse in any way he can.

At 8 A.M. Sunday morning, Dean Richardson was on a US Airways flight as it lifted off the runway at a Palm Beach airport, bound for Philadelphia. He is tough, but he is human. On the other hand, he knew that this is why he became a veterinarian, this is why he became a surgeon, why he became a doctor. This, really, was what being a doctor was all about. Tomorrow, he knew, the world watching, he would walk into the operating room and try to save Barbaro's life.

. . . about as difficult as an operation could be.—**Dr. Dean Richardson**

The
Operation

12

Dr. Richardson arrived at the hospital at around noon. His intention was to go into the hospital, perform the operation, and then talk to the mass media that had gathered. But they were so hungry for something that Richardson and Dr. Barbara Dallap, an emergency clinician who had been one of the doctors waiting for Barbaro when he arrived at New Bolton, stood in front of an overflowing crowd in the A meeting room before the surgery, and he laid out his strategy.

He was in good humor at the meeting. In response to one reporter who asked him, "When will you begin the surgery?" he quipped, "As soon as you stop asking me questions."

Then he answered some more questions and prepared for surgery, and began. Barbaro was put under general anesthesia by Dr. Ben Driessen, assisted by residents Dr. Liberty Gutman, Dr. Steve Zedler, and Dr. David Levine, and the operation began. It was a complex surgery. Richardson later said. "Barbaro presented a case that was about as difficult as an operation could be."

Working deliberately and watching Barbaro's vital signs, the doctors opened him up and started to reassemble his shattered bones, and it was here that Richardson's great hands lived up to their reputation. One by one, he reassembled the bones with titanium screws, or implants, as they're known in surgery, and a plate, driving the screws through and into the plate.

The operation went smoothly, but Richardson found it particularly difficult to fit some of the pieces of bone snugly so he could then drive the implants in and hold them together. As it happened, at one point, Barbaro had rubbed the broken limb so much that he had smoothed out some of the bones and they no longer fit together well. Richardson had to transplant some bone from the horse's hip to achieve this. When he was finished, the leg was put in a cast.

When the operation was over, it was obviously a success, but there was still great danger for Barbaro simply because he was an animal. One can't say, "Look, Barbaro, we just finished reassembling your leg, so when you wake up from anesthesia, don't thrash

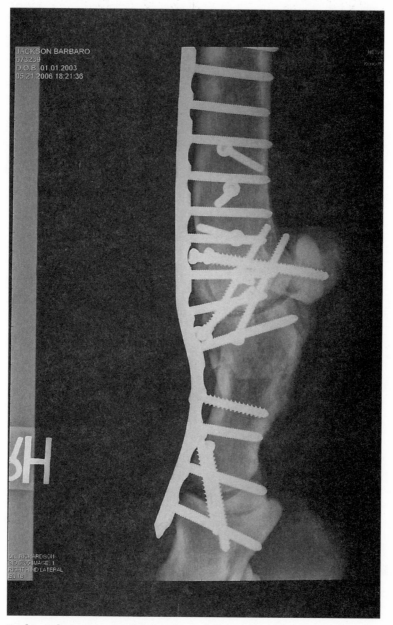

Barbaro's leg was reassembled with more than 20 screws—and a plate.

around and possibly rebreak the leg and ruin the operation, okay?"

He was, of course, in the ICU and would be kept under virtually constant observation. Also, a horse coming out of an operation may well be disoriented and panicky and will thrash around when he wakes up. Happily, New Bolton was ready for this. To keep him from hurting himself, he was put in a harness and carried by monorail so he was above a pool of warm water covered by a rubber raft with four holes in it for his legs. Then he was carefully lowered so the legs went through the holes into the warm water. If he moved them when he awoke, they would churn harmlessly through the warm water.

The system worked wonderfully for Barbaro, and he got through the recovery procedure without reinjuring himself. He was outfitted with a fiberglass cast, and when he was fully mobile, said Dr. Richardson, he "practically jogged back to his stall."

Literally overnight, there was, of course, tremendous interest in Barbaro. And on May 23, two days after the surgery, reporters gathered in an auditorium in the hospital with the Jacksons and Dr. Richardson, who would answer all questions. Dr. Richardson immediately reassured everyone that Barbaro was doing fine. Indeed, he provided the telling example that he was not only walking well with the new cast but "actually was scratching his left ear with his left hind leg, which is his good leg." And how could the doctors tell? There were objective signs—temperature, pulse, respiration, attitude, appetite—but Richardson said that you could also tell simply by looking into Barbaro's eyes. Anyone who knows horses also knows that you can tell how a horse is doing by looking into his eyes.

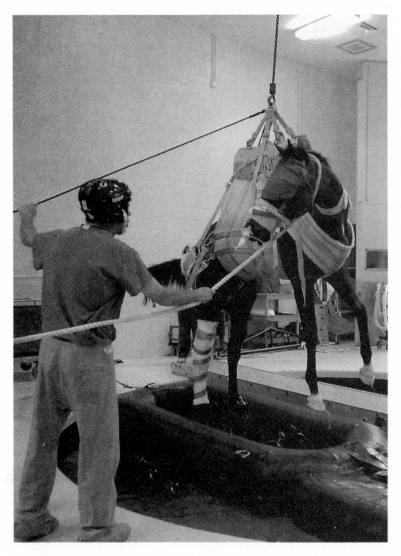

The sling was very helpful in lowering Barbaro into water while he was recovering from surgery, and to keep weight off his legs.

The main concern now was possible "complications," and to avoid them, Barbaro would have his right hind leg in a cast indefinitely. Richardson explained that the screws and plate to reassemble his leg "are not adequate. . . . to allow him to bear weight without a cast. There are many types of surgical repairs that we do in which the plates and screws are enough to hold things together. This is far too complicated a fracture for that. So we need to keep him in the cast as well."

But there danger lurks, because, as said before, one is dealing with an animal, not a human being. You can't tell him, as you would a person, to be calm as you change his cast, so the hospital put Barbaro in a sling and mildly sedated him and then changed the cast. However, if he started getting rambunctious—then, Richardson, they would put him under general anesthesia and wake him up immersed in the pool, as they did after the operation.

Perhaps the main question in everyone's mind pertained to complications. One of these was the standard problem, after human or animal surgery, of infection. But there were other problems that could be brought about by excess weight. Barbaro might tend to bear most of his weight on his good leg because the cast on the injured one extended down and prevented him from exerting weight on it. The other leg could develop problems because of this extra weight.

But, Richardson said, "as long as he's comfortable, this is less likely to occur. In terms of what is being done to prevent this, when he came in, his racing shoes were removed altogether—his left hind foot was shod with a special glue-on shoe that had special padding. It also raises his foot up a little bit so that his limb length

He ate well throughout his hospitalization.

is equivalent to the cast limb on the right hind. So he has a special shoe in place."

Another concern was whether Barbaro would be able to breed other little Barbaros if and when he got well. Richardson said that that was far down the road, but was possible, though it could be problematic because in breeding, a sire has to stand on his rear legs to mount the mare and, here again, pressure would be put on the repaired leg, which would have to be able to bear weight.

In horse breeding, many people are surprised to hear that artificial insemination is not allowed. Breeding must be done by what Sue McDonnell of the Equine Behavior Laboratory says is "natural service; artificial insemination and assisted reproductive techniques are not allowed." However, there are methods to help disabled stallions get the job done, ranging from custom-built breeding ramps to supportive splints or casts to medications that reduce the amount of effort required, and skilled people who can help the stallion to compensate for its limitations.

It has been suggested that breeding was the real reason the Jacksons wanted Barbaro to survive, that his stud fee would have gone through the roof. Dean Richardson took the opportunity to set the record straight, partly because he had misspoken after coming out of surgery. "I made a point about how the optimal outcome for the horse is that he be salvaged for breeding. And some people are taking that the wrong way. I want everyone to understand that if this horse were a gelding, these owners would have definitely done everything to save this horse's life. I know the Jacksons a long time. This horse could have no reproductive value, and they would have saved this horse's life."

To the Jacksons and Richardson, saving the horse's life meant that he could return to a life on the farm—his racing career was over, of course—pain free, comfortable. As Gretchen Jackson said, he has to be able "to live a good-quality life."

Richardson said it would be months before they would discharge Barbaro from the hospital. And he made it quite clear that Barbaro was far from "out of the woods." Richardson explained that Barbaro was a 1,200-pound animal and that complications could occur—all kinds of complications—over the next few weeks, though he did not say what they were.

Bombshell

*T*hings seemed to be going well for Barbaro. In the week following the May 23 news conference, he ate well, his bodily functions were fine, he had a great attitude, he was not in pain because of the medication he was taking, and in general, Dr. Richardson was very pleased. What is more, he was being well fed—and then some. Twice a day, volunteers,

13

of which there was no shortage, would handpick grass from the pasture outside the hospital and feed it to him.

The Jacksons visited him daily, and he also got some treats from them, with Gretchen feeding him carrots and Roy feeding him mints, which he actually ate, contrary to when he was growing up on Sanborn Chase Farm, where they tried to feed him peppermints but he wouldn't eat them, said Sanborn night watchman Irvin White.

On May 30, when his schedule allowed him, Edgar Prado, a very emotional man, visited Barbaro, and if anyone had ever doubted how Prado felt about the horse, they should have witnessed the reunion, which brought tears not only to Prado's eyes but to those of the people watching the reunion. The connection was there and would always be there.

June 10, 2006, was a somewhat sad day, though it had nothing to do with Barbaro's health. A horse named "Jazil" won the Belmont Stakes, but if you closed your eyes you could envision what might have happened. Jazil might have been looking at the rapidly disappearing rump of Barbaro. Instead, the great horse was in his stall at New Bolton.

The medical care continued, but, as Dr. Richardson characterized it, it consisted mostly of nursing care, in which Barbaro was washed, given his medication, walked, had bandages changed, and the like.

Then, on June 13, a little more than three weeks after Barbaro had first received it, Dr. Richardson did something that might not have seemed dramatic but was: He replaced the cast on the horse's leg. Doing this not only allowed the medical team to put on the new, necessary cast but to get a clearer idea of how the bones were healing—radiographs didn't penetrate the cast that well. One word described Dr. Richardson's reaction: "Excellent!"

Barbaro continued to be characterized as a very good patient. Some horses create problems when they're in a hospital, but Barbaro demonstrated the same intelligence he had always had and was able to engage only in activities that were in his own self-interest. Richardson was very pleased with Barbaro's progress. Said Richardson around June 20: "He's a lively, bright, happy horse. If you asked me a month ago, I would have gladly accepted where we are today."

But again—and again—anyone listening to anything about Barbaro knew quite well that things could take a turn for the worst. What most people didn't know, however, was how quickly they could take that wrong turn.

Barbaro continued to do well, but on July 5, it was necessary to replace the cast not as part of normal procedure but because two of the screws, or implants, had bent and three new screws had to be implanted in the pastern bone. Then Barbaro experienced some discomfort with the new cast, and on July 5, the cast was replaced yet again. He also had developed an abscess on his left hind foot, and this had to be treated.

He was, again, being watched 24 hours a day—this was ICU for a horse—and the people in the facility are top notch. Though there are objective tests for telling how well a patient is doing or if there are any difficulties, one nurse said, "You can tell if a horse is in pain or difficulty—most animals, for that matter—by just looking in their eyes. Particularly a horse, and particularly Barbaro. He has big, soulful eyes."

Throughout all his treatment, Barbaro continued to receive the

The Jacksons meet with the distraught Edgar Prado.

love and good wishes that people felt for him. The hospital had established a special e-mail contact address—perhaps he is the only horse who has an e-mail address—and it collected endless messages. And gifts, flowers, and the like continued to pour in.

But nothing, really, could fill the occasional empty feeling in, as it were, the belly of America. People were clearly very tense about Barbaro's condition. The typical comment you heard at the time was "Oh, I'm sure he'll be fine." The only problem that you had as a listener was that you had a hard time believing it, because you knew that the person who told it to you was also having trouble believing it.

In early July, the weather got very hot, as it almost always does, and the rumors started to get hot as well that Barbaro was having some difficulty, complications. In fact, the rumors were true. On

July 10, the cast was replaced yet again, this time with a shorter one, but Barbaro had a fever and was in some discomfort. Then Dr. Richardson made an ominous statement during a television interview to the effect that he believed there was going to be some "tough days" ahead but did not specify what he had seen. They were tough days indeed.

On the evening of July 12, Richardson called the Jacksons and Michael Matz to a meeting. He told them that Barbaro had come down with one of the complications that Dean feared most . . . laminitis. And it wasn't a mild form of the disease. It was, Richardson said, "as bad as it gets." It was clearly life-threatening, something that Roy Jackson's tears bespoke eloquently. The question the Jacksons and Matz had to face was whether or not Barbaro should be put down, euthanized.

As long-time horsemen, the Jacksons and Matz knew all about laminitis. An object lesson was what the great horse Secretariat had been through, having had it. In 1973, with Ron Turcotte aboard, Secretariat, or "Big Red," rode to a decisive victory in the Kentucky Derby, the first horse ever to run the distance in under two minutes. Then he won the Preakness, and then the Belmont Stakes by—gulp—31 lengths and became, of course, the Triple Crown winner.

The horse was lauded, and even today he is remembered and honored. Recently in 2005, on ESPN's Classic's show *Who's No. 1 in the List* of "Greatest Sports Performances" individual athletes, Secretariat was the only nonhuman on the list for his 31-length Belmont victory, ranking second only to Wilt Chamberlain's 100-point game.

Secretariat was retired to Claiborne Farm in Kentucky by his owner, Penny Chenery, when he was three, and for many years he was an outstanding stud. And then, at the age of nineteen, he came down with the very painful disease laminitis in all four hoofs. In this disease, connecting tissue from four bones to the hoof becomes inflamed and the horse can't stand without extreme pain. Or, as one vet described, picture yourself having a door slam on an index finger, then having to put your full body weight on the finger to support yourself.

It was the same disease that Barbaro had acquired, and nothing was dreaded more by horsemen. A press conference was called for the next day. Dr. Richardson, dressed in his blue surgical garb—because he was to perform a couple of surgeries—was very much more downbeat than he had been at the first press conference. He sat down at the table in front of a cluster of microphones and answered questions from the press. And chances are that almost everyone in the room had a single thought: Barbaro was going to die, or maybe he was already dead. Richardson would inform them.

He began the conference in his usual straightforward manner. "We have been trying to be very straightforward with the public about what's going on with the horse. We've pointed out that the horse had some major complications in the last week and the reason I wanted to address a larger group is because he's had even more serious complications in the last couple of days. The most feared complication from the outset for this horse was that he would develop laminitis in his good foot. And the horse has suffered an acute, rather severe bout of laminitis in his left hind foot."

Then he explained what had happened. Barbaro had started to have some trouble in the fractured leg at around week seven—the

Press conference. Dr. Richardson made the announcement about the dreaded laminitis.

first days of July—and he started to support his weight on his left foot, which led to the stress, despite the special shoe, and then, just like that, laminitis came—quickly and savagely.

The damage was severe. The laminae are the flexible strands that connect the horse's bottom bone in his foot—called the coffin bone—to the inside of the hoof. When the laminae get inflamed, they gradually lose their grip on the inside of the hoof.

In Barbaro's case, the degree of damage was described by Richardson as being as "bad as it gets" because 80 percent of the laminae had let go, with only 20 percent still attached to the hoof. Richardson explained that for this reason, after discussion with the Jacksons, a "hoof wall resection" of that loosened 80 percent of the laminae was done because they were no longer functioning. Was Barbaro going to be euthanized? Richardson said the bottom line

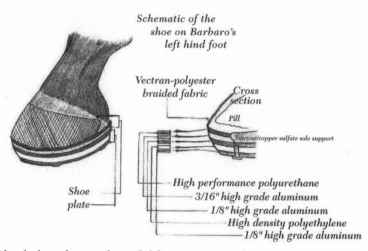

Schematic of the
shoe on Barbaro's
left hind foot

Vectran-polyester
braided fabric

Cross
section

Pill

Silicone/copper sulfate sole support

Shoe
plate

High performance polyurethane
3/16" high grade aluminum
1/8" high grade aluminum
High density polyethylene
1/8" high grade aluminum

Sketch shows how Barbaro's left leg was supported.

was that the horse's comfort had diminished, and that, ultimately, was the main criterion for the Jacksons. If he couldn't live a life in comfort, then he would be euthanized.

And most people in the room probably sensed, from Richardson's explanation and tone, that that would happen, though of course it had not happened yet. Barbaro was taking heavy doses of pain medication—epidurals, which block pain in humans from the waist down and are frequently used in childbirth—and so far the painkiller was working, as far as they could tell. When someone approached, Richardson said, Barbaro "nickers at them." He was still eating well. He had excellent GI function, was managing his weight, his heart rate was low and his temperatures back to normal after the previous surgery. And of course, there were those eyes.

But, the doctor said, ominously, "We are only going to go on with this horse as long as everyone involved is convinced that on that day and the next day he is going to be acceptably comfortable."

People started firing questions at him, but the essential one was, could he get better? Richardson's answer was yes, but the only way that could happen was if Barbaro grew new laminae, which also could happen, a process that could take months. And meanwhile, there could be a new outbreak of laminitis. Richardson said that bad things tend to happen very quickly, while good things "take a long time to occur."

When asked to put a percentage on Barbaro's chances of recovering, Richardson said he didn't want to, but he did characterize it as "poor." Of course, when Barbaro first fractured his leg, Richardson said his chances were only fifty-fifty. But Richardson said he could recover, and as long as Barbaro wasn't suffering, then "we're going to continue to try. We think that if we can keep him comfortable, it's worth the effort."

Someone asked if Barbaro was likely to get laminitis in his right foot. Richardson was blunt: "It's possible, absolutely. And if he were to develop it in another foot, we would not continue." But Dr. Richardson said that the right leg was doing fine, healing well.

"If you asked me two weeks ago . . . I really thought we were going to make it two weeks ago."

But now, obviously, he didn't, and the sense was that everyone was on a death watch. This was one race that Barbaro could not win.

But then again, the words of trainer Alan Jerkens echoed in the mind of one of the authors of this book: "The only thing you know for certain is that you know nothing for certain."

"A Miracle in Progress"

*F*ollowing the news conference on July 13, people who were rooting for Barbaro were gripped with more fear and apprehension than at any time since the ordeal began. Most people were waiting for him to die or, more to the point, be euthanized. After all, the original odds on his surviving were fifty-fifty and plummeted after that. The Jacksons had made

14

clear that before Barbaro would be allowed to suffer, he would be put down. Barbaro would not suffer.

One can only surmise how much pain the Jacksons were suffering. Who knew whether the next phone call would be one from New Bolton telling them to come to the hospital, that the pain had gotten unendurable for Barbaro and that it was time to say goodbye.

Indeed, the pain could get unendurable. The disease had caused Secretariat so much pain that he had actually screamed. If anything could put in perspective what the doctors at New Bolton were dealing with, it was the horrific death of that great horse Secretariat.

So all anyone could do was wait—wait for what looked like the inevitable. Many people expected him to pass within a day or two, but on July 14, the hospital issued another medical bulletin on his condition: "Barbaro was out of his sling for more than twelve hours yesterday, and he had a calm, restful night, sleeping on his side for more than four hours," reported Dr. Richardson.

The sling had proved useful during Barbaro's entire hospitalization, but it was not particularly useful. The horse could be put in it and held suspended above the floor so he would not weigh down on his hooves, particularly the laminitic one. Unfortunately, he could not stay in the sling more than a few hours or it could lead to other problems.

But Dr. Richardson still had to give caution: "While his condition is stable, it remains extremely serious. His vital signs, including heart rate and pulse, remain good. We are treating his laminitis aggressively and he continues to respond well and is acceptably comfortable.

"As I said at the press conference on Thursday, we monitor his condition very closely because signs can change quickly." But he also emphasized that Barbaro, as evident in the film footage and still photos released, had a very positive attitude.

A number of fans who were asked about how they felt about the news were still downbeat, but one man said, "What I like about what they're doing is fighting the laminitis. You always feel better when you fight back."

No news is good news, and July 13 and 14 passed uneventfully. People went about their business, but every now and then, Barbaro galloped, as it were, through their minds. A new bulletin came out of the hospital on July 15, and the news was good.

"Barbaro's vital signs are good and he had another quiet, restful night. He remains in stable condition, and he is eating well," said Dr. Richardson. "We continue to manage his pain successfully, and he is alert. It is important for people to understand that this is not a 'routine' laminitis. The care involved in treating a hoof with this degree of compromise is complex."

Again, as always, Dr. Richardson had included his little caveat, his little caution, but who wouldn't, in his position. Said one vet, "Who, indeed, would want to be in his position, the main person responsible for the life of a horse that untold thousands of people had grown to love? Not me."

Of course, Richardson had said at the beginning that when he operated on Barbaro, it wouldn't be Barbaro but just a horse who needed an operation, even if it were some ancient gelding.

Another bulletin was issued on July 18. "I knew he was okay," said Scott Baker, a big fan of Barbaro. "This guy I know named Ed Lindstadt in Northport knows all about it, and somehow it's easier getting the news from him than the Internet. So that's the way I get it. The doctors did a lot."

THE NEWS ON BARBARO FROM JULY 18, 2006—"Yesterday afternoon we changed his right-hind-leg cast to take new radiographs and to examine the incision. The radiographs looked good; the plates we placed on July 8 to fuse the pastern are intact and the fetlock fusion is unchanged. The leg and the incision looked as good as we could have hoped. The modified foot cast, which acts like a bandage on Barbaro's left hind foot, was also changed yesterday.

"The foot cast is rigid and provides stability and support but will be changed often so that the hoof can be treated. Both cast changes were performed with Barbaro lightly sedated in a sling. He has adapted very well to being managed as needed in the sling. He is a very intelligent horse."

ON JULY 19, ANOTHER BULLETIN WAS ISSUED—"Barbaro spends several hours a day in a sling which he has adapted to very well."

And then another:

JULY 20, 2006—"His vital signs are good and his attitude remains positive. He slept well and is comfortable this morning."

A week passed, and the good news continued, and on July 21 they issued another bulletin, also good:

JULY 21, 2006—"He had another restful night and his vital signs are good," said Dr. Richardson. "We continue to monitor him closely and he is responding as well as can be expected to treatment."

Look, it was July 21 and Barbaro was still going! Wasn't he supposed to be gone by now? Wasn't he? Well, he isn't.

Another bulletin was issued on the 24th, and again a lot had been done to Barbaro. But the big news, the very hopeful news, was that he was out of his sling and sleeping in his stall! ("And who the hell likes to sleep in a sling?" Joe Beck said.)

JULY 24, 2006—"He's maintaining an excellent attitude," said Dr. Richardson. "We change his left-hind-foot cast regularly, and we may change his right-hind cast some time this week. He is out of the sling overnight because he is very smart about lying down and sleeping. He continues to eat a diet designed to maximize protein and caloric intake, and his body condition is good for a horse that has had (and is having) his problems. His diet includes a selection of the best-quality hay."

On July 26 came another bulletin, and no one could accuse the hospital of not being on top of keeping the world informed.

JULY 26—"Barbaro slept well after his left-hind-foot bandage was changed yesterday," said Dr. Richardson. "I'm happy with the appearance of this foot, which is doing as well as can be expected. Over the last several days, his temperature has been normal and his bloodwork has significantly improved, suggesting that the infection in his right hind foot is under control. His heart rate is also consistently normal now, a good indication that he is stable and comfortable."

JULY 28, 2006—"He continues to be stable after another comfortable night. His right-hind-leg cast was changed late Wednesday. We took new radiographs, and they look good. No problems were evident. The modified foot cast on Barbaro's left hind foot, which has laminitis, is changed daily so the foot can be treated and watched for signs of infection. Barbaro has a strong appetite and he has been enjoying hand-picked grass daily and 'healthy snacks.' "

And then, July was gone And he was still here.
And a little survey showed that a lot of
people were starting to have more hope.

AUGUST 1, 2006—"Barbaro's condition continues to be stable," said Dr. Richardson. "We changed his left-hind-foot bandage daily, and it looks good. His right hind leg also looks good, and his appetite remains strong."

And then, on August 3, a bulletin came forth that made Barbaro fans a little giddy. It was truly a very positive sign. Dr. Richardson had said that for Barbaro to survive, the laminae would have to grow back. They were doing just that! Hallelujah!

AUGUST 3, 2006—"The left hind hoof is slowly showing evidence of regrowth. The coronary band [the portion of the hoof that is responsible for continued downward growth] is beginning to reestablish itself."

A couple of days later there was more good news:

AUGUST 5, 2006—"The original fractures [of the right hind leg] have apparently healed well, but the cast is necessary to protect the pastern fusion. This protection is required because he must bear most of his weight on the right hind limb due to the laminitis in the left hind leg."

The August 8th bulletin showed more regrowth:

AUGUST 8, 2006—"Changing the cast [of the right hind foot] gives us the opportunity to take new radiographs and evaluate the progress of the fracture healing and joint fusions. His left hind hoof continues to show signs of regrowth and looks healthy. And he has a daily bandage change for examination and treatment."

It had now been almost a month since the dire news about the laminitis, and Barbaro was still rolling along.

AUGUST 9, 2006—[After removing his cast] "The leg looked good under the cast, especially considering the length of time that he has been in a cast. There is no sign of active infection. This is further supported by his markedly improving blood values over the last two weeks. He had an excellent pool recovery; he is a very intelligent horse and has definitely figured out the whole process. The appearance of the [left hind] foot is very good. It is dry and healthy looking with excellent early regrowth at the coronary band."

The August 22 bulletin spoke for itself.

AUGUST 22, 2006—"Barbaro is doing well on both hind limbs. Because of this, we do not plan to change his right hind cast in the next two weeks. He needs to continue to improve over the next few months before we will have a better idea about his long-term comfort. Barbaro's appetite and his attitude right now are phenomenal; he attacks his feed and when he goes out to graze, he acts like he thinks he could train. Right now, he is a surprisingly happy horse. He is gaining weight and has had his pain medications reduced without any effect on his well-being. His strength and overall appearance have been improving since he became well enough to be walked outside each day."

AUGUST 28, 2006—"The cast was changed because there was a small crack in it. "Based on new radiographs that were taken, the leg looked excellent under the cast. The pastern joint looks completely fused, and there is only a small area in the long pastern bone that has a little farther to go before we take him out of the cast completely."

August was gone. And he is still here.

SEPTEMBER 5, 2006—"Barbaro is wearing the new cast satisfactorily," said Dr. Richardson. "We continue to monitor him closely, and depending on how he progresses, we may change it again within the next two weeks. Barbaro's appetite is great, and we take him out each day to hand-graze him. His vital signs remain normal, and he seems very happy."

SEPTEMBER 12, 2006—"We are pleased with his progress. He is wearing the cast on his right hind limb well; we continue to monitor it closely, and we expect to change the cast and radiograph the leg within the next seven to ten days. The left hind foot is progressing well, especially as it grows down from the coronary band. However, we remain cautious, because Barbaro will still need several more months of healing before we'll know how well the overall hoof structure can be restored."

SEPTEMBER 19, 2006—"He had an excellent week. We replaced the boot on his left hind foot with a bandage because the hoof is doing well. He is enjoying his daily excursions outside to graze, and his appetite is excellent."

One fan described the September 26 bulletin as "phenomenal."

SEPTEMBER 26, 2006—"The left hind hoof on Barbaro has grown about eighteen millimeters in the heel area. It has to grow at least three times that, which could take more than six months. It's a very gradual process; the bottom of his foot has to completely heal as well. As always, we monitor his comfort very closely, and we will likely change the cast within the next two weeks. Barbaro's vital signs continue to be excellent, as is his appetite. He definitely

Many people waited for Barbaro to die, but Yogi Berra's line came to mind, "It's not over till it's over," and soon Barbaro was outside eating grass with the ever-watchful Dr. Richardson.

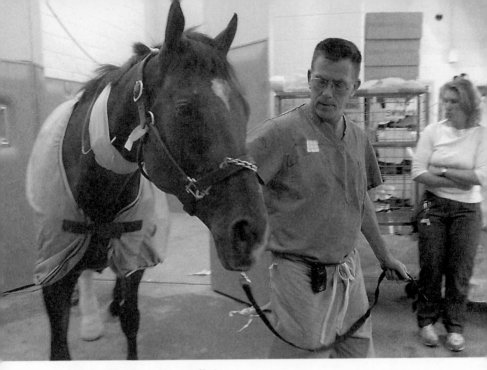

He also likes his indoor walks!

enjoys his daily thirty- to forty-minute excursions outside to walk and graze."

September was gone. And he's still here.

OCTOBER 3, 2006—"He is doing very, very well. His appetite and vital signs continue to be excellent."

OCTOBER 10, 2006—"We placed Barbaro under general anesthesia to remove the old cast on his right hind limb and took new radiographs to assess the continued healing of the original injuries. I was pleased with the continued progression of healing and the overall condition of this leg. There are no signs of infection and the primary incisions have healed surprisingly well. Because he has had a cast on for so long, there are a few cast sores, but nothing serious. [On the left hind foot] there is good growth along the quarters [closer to the heel], but there will need to be much more healing along the front of the hoof. We still have many months of healing ahead of us."

OCTOBER 17, 2006—"Barbaro is wearing his new cast comfortably and his vital signs and appetite remain excellent. The [left hind] hoof is growing slowly, but he has a long way to go, especially along the front of the hoof. We still have many months of healing ahead of us. The foot will require meticulous care for a long time."

Now the reports were coming a week apart, though fans agreed that this one was just a tad scary.

OCTOBER 24, 2006—"I am happy to report that Barbaro had another good week, and his appetite and vital signs remain excellent. We are being very conservative [keeping it in a cast] with the right hind [fractured] limb in order to help protect the foundered left hind foot. The hoof is growing slowly and not uniformly, so it has a long way to go before it is acceptably strong and functional. The foot will require meticulous care for a long time and setbacks here and there are probable."

Adiós, October, Barbaro's still here.

NOVEMBER 2, 2006—"Barbaro had radiographs taken through his fiberglass cast on November 1. The healing appears substantial enough that we plan to remove his cast and replace it with a splinted bandage some time next week We will take some more radiographs after his cast is removed under general anesthesia. He will then be recovered again using our swimming pool system."

NOVEMBER 6, 2006—"Barbaro was placed under general anesthesia for the cast removal from his right hind leg. In addition, his foot was trimmed and a new shoe glued on. A padded bandage with plastic and fiberglass splints was placed on his lower limb for support. He had a perfect pool recovery and immediately stood; he walked easily back to his stall. He used all of his legs quite well. There are no signs of new problems with that foot, but the hoof needs several more months of growth before we will know how much foot structure and function will be recovered."

So now, six months after the world waited for him to die, he's still here. He had, thus far, survived a bout of laminitis that was, as Dr. Richardson said, "as bad as it gets." But he has a good chance of surviving, period. Miracles do happen, and this, as Roy Jackson said, "is a miracle in progress."

Amen.

SLINGS

Slings, which were originally designed for rescuing horses, are now common in the treatment of those with conditions that include neurological problems or musculoskeletal injuries. They have been in use for many years for long-term management of a horse's movement. "We have a lot of experience in using slings for equine support," said Dr. Richardson. "In Barbaro's case, it is a part-time aid that we use to increase his comfort level."

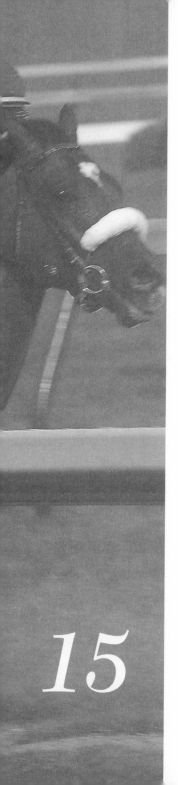

15

"Grow Hoof Grow!" and Other Love Letters to Barbaro

Since Barbaro broke down, there has been, as mentioned before, an incredible response to his predicament and condition, an outpouring of love, particularly via the Internet, that is wonderful to behold. There have been tens of thousands of messages, short and long, sent by all kinds of people from all walks of life and every nook and cranny in America.

Happily, the University of Pennsylvania Veterinary School, at whose facility (the George D. Widener Hospital for Large Animals) Barbaro was treated, has published many of these.

Following is a tiny selection of messages, a drop in the bucket and huge in implication—namely, that there are still wonderful people out there who love a fellow creature so much. To all those people we say: Thank you. You are, in the immortal words of Jackie Gleason, "The Greatest!"

"Dear Mr. and Mrs. Jackson,

I just wanted to tell you a story that may help you bear up under all that you are going through, and I know that you are going through a lot. In fact, I admire you very much for going through everything with Barbaro, because my family and I had a similar choice. It was a cat named Ludwig, but it had been with our family for a long time, loved by me and my sister and my brother and my parents all loved this cat—he was an indoor cat—for ten years. But one day he started to have some symptoms, and we took him to the vet—he was a lot different than your vet—and he told us that the cat was suffering from a par virus. And that we only had two choices: 'aspirate fluid from his lungs or put him down.'

Our instinct was to fight for his life, and we did, but only one place told us they could help us and that would cost us thousands of dollars.

"We didn't have that kind of money, didn't know what to do. Then I said: What place is likely to be able to help us, and I thought: A college. So we called up the vet school at Cornell and got a vet on the phone named Jeff Barlow, and when we explained what was wrong he asked: 'How is the cat, is he comatose?' I said no. And then he said: 'Okay, he'll be fine.' We asked what he meant and he said that that if the vet continued to do what he did he'd be fine. And he was! The vet started

At Belmont Park, a sign sixty feet long was made.

calling him the miracle cat, but it wasn't a miracle, it was just our instinct to not let him die so easy.

> GOOD LUCK.
> MARY KIM
> EAST HAMPTON, NY"

"Grow Hoof Grow!

> AMIE, GRAND RAPIDS, MICHIGAN"

"Good Morning Beautiful Boy. I mention you each day in my prayers, never thought I'd be praying for a horse, but you are special. You have shown great strength and courage—traits we all should have. We love you. Stay strong.

> OUIDA, R.N.; NORWALK, CA, USA"

We almost forgot Barbaro's favorite profile shot. Here it is!

"Hi Sweet boy—just my daily note to tell you I love you—hope you have a good weekend. Tons of hugs & kisses.

DEBBIE, CARROLLTON, TX"

"Hiddeehoe Sweet Boy! Wonderful wonderful wonderful! *SMMMMWAAAAH*

LOVE, AUNTIE RUTH, DURHAM"

"Great news Big B! Keep up the good work everyone. Keep hanging in there big guy and have a wonderful weekend!

JANE, 42, MAMERS, NC"

"GLAD TO HEAR YOU ARE DOING SO GREAT. I SAY A
GOOD THOUGHT FOR YOU EVERY DAY. KEEP ON GETTING
WELL

> BARBARA, 68, BUMPASS, VA, USA"

"DEAREST ONE, HAVE A GREAT WEEKEND AND KEEP WORK-
ING & PROTECTING THOSE LEGS.

> LOVE & KISSES
> DEB, 48, SPRING VALLEY, MN"

"Deep love and my prayers are being sent for your speedy recovery.
Godspeed Barbaro.

> RHONDA, RI"

"Hang in there—I'm praying for you!

> DAVE, TORONTO, CANADA"

"Sweet Barbaro, so very happy to hear such good news again about
you! Have a wonderful, healthy weekend with lots of treats and grazing time. We love you!

> GAIL AND THE FURRY 15
> AND FEATHERED
> GAIL, 57, MARYVILLE, TN, USA"

"Hi Sweet Prince! Something told me to wish you well . . . right now. I
hope you are having a good day. Listen to the doctors.

> XOXOXO CANDY, 46, MOUND, MN,
> USA"

"Barbaro, I am so happy to hear of your continuing progress. You are a true champion. I look at your pictures and wish I could see you some day. Hopefully, I can. You're a gorgeous boy! Take care. The fillies are waiting!

BARBARA, 51, IL"

"BARBARO . . . I CHECK IN ON YOU AT EVERY UPDATE & IT'S A JOY TO HEAR THAT YOU ARE DOING SO GOOD . . . I KNOW YOU LIKE YOUR GRAZING OUTSIDE & PLEASE KEEP GETTING BETTER . . . KEEP EATING TOO!!! HAVE A NICE WEEKEND.

LOVE ME.

LENORE, 50; PHILADELPHIA, PA"

"Hi Handsome Sweetheart :) Happy Friday to you and yours! I hope you have a wonderful weekend, filled with love, good treaties, more love and LOTS of healing. Be strong . . . be careful o'side. 'See' you on Monday! I love you!

XOXOXOXOXO

LYNNE, 61, SONORA, CA, USA"

"Another week and you look great. Bravo to the Jacksons for their determination. Bravo to the staff and doctors, especially Dr. Richardson, for looking after you. Thanks to God for the miracle.

LINDA, 61, KNOXVILLE, TN."

"Barbaro—Have a great weekend! My daily Rosary continues your Miracle! Hope you get blessed for 10-4-St. Francis Feast. Thank you, Dr. Dean, the Jacksons, NBC, UPenn, and Team Barbaro! Keep fightin'/healin'.

LINDA, 45, PEORIA, IL, USA"

"Hi Beautiful Barbaro, Hope You Have A Wonderful + Restful Weekend. Keep Having Your Fighting Spirit + Great Appetite. You Are An
Inspiration To The World. Love, Thoughts + Prayers.

> *ALWAYS, GILLIAN + TUPPY WOOF XOX*
> *TUPPY + GILLIAN, 44, VICTORIA,*
> *BRITISH COLUMBIA, CANADA"*

"I check quite often on Barbaro's condition. He has stolen my heart!
Thanks to all the wonderful care you give him everyday. I pray he
keeps on getting better. God Bless you all.

> *BARBARA, CLEARWATER, FL, USA"*

"Wishing you another feel good, feel fine and grow that hoof kind of
weekend. Stay as smart as you are and although you may feel like kick-
ing up your heels—please don't. LOVE YOU TO PIECES!!!

> *SHIRLEY-ANN, 75, KETTERING, OH,*
> *USA"*

"Dear Beautiful Barbaro, sending my wish to you and Dr. Dean and
staff, your family, jockey, trainer for a restful, healing, happy weekend.
Prayers always and love to you!

> *JILL, 51, GREEN VALLEY, AZ, USA*
> *XOXO"*

"Dear Barbaro, so happy to hear your latest update. You are a warrior,
that's for sure. Be good to all your caretakers—they must love you a
ton. Eat lots of grass this weekend and get plenty of rest.

> *LOVE, KATHLEEN*
> *LOCUST, NC, USA"*

"BARBARO! Sweetie, it's the w/end again. Hope URs is filled with happiness. Be good & take care! I'm sending prayers 2 U 4 Ur health & comfort. I'm also praying for Dr. R. C'ya Monday.

HORSIE HUGS & KISSES!

CATHY, 44, NJ"

"Sweet brave Barbaro—I wish you a restful, comfortable weekend. Your pictures bring a smile. You're inspirational! Your doctors, wonderful—much admired. God bless—keep healing! Prayers!

PAT, ANNAPOLIS"

"So happy to hear that you are doing wonderfully. Keep up your spirits, Barbaro. You are a true Champion. Thanks to Dr. Richardson, his staff and Mr. and Mrs. Jackson. I love you champ.

BARBARA, PORT ST. LUCIE, FL, USA"

"Hey Boy How you doing? Just a few lines to let you know I'm thinking and praying for you like everyone else. You'll be okay, your in God's hands, Lots of Love Keep up the good work.

LOVE YOU OXOXOX

CHANDLER, GLEN BURNIE, MD,

USA"

"Good morning Big B—it's a beautiful crisp fall day—hope you are able to go out and feel the sun on your back. Glad to hear ACN—you've conquered yet another week. Cooper sends "woofs" & I send you love & scratchies.

SYLVIA & COOPER (WOOF); ONTARIO,

CANADA"

"Hey big guy, sooo happy that u r continuing to improve & grow that hoof, happy that u r going outside soon green pastures for u hugs & kisses.

CATHI, ENGLEWOOD, FL, USA"

"Barbaro dear, just dropping in to wish you a beautiful sunny, breezy autumn weekend. May you continue to enjoy the outdoors, but remember . . . easy on your feet. All our prayers and love!

JENNY"

"Hi Barbaro: Have a great weekend. You are a young horse and you have a good life ahead of you. Be patient: we are all pulling for you.

CHRISTINA, FONTANA, CA, USA"

"BARBARO! O, NO! 2-day's Fri. again. & U no what THAT means! 2 LONGG days w/out hearing from U Sweetie, enjoy the w/e, & no I am praying 4 Ur health & happiness nonstop. I luv U, Barbaro. C'ya Monday!

CATHY, NJ"

"God Bless you, Sweetheart! Have a peaceful, healing and comfortable day, and weekend. We love you!

FRAN, SCHENECTADY, NY"

"Good Morning! Thinking about you and hoping you are feeling good. I am proud of you and the doctors who are taking care of you.

LOVE YA!

LINDA, LEE'S SUMMIT, JACKSON, MO"

"Hey Barbaro, I hope you have a wonderful restful weekend. Rest is so important to your healing. Continuing to pray for your recovery. Mind your wonderful Doctors. You are such a magnificent horse! Take care.

LOVE

DIANE, CHARLOTTE, NC, USA"

"Keep getting better . . . and for the owners and the vets, I have my fingers crossed for a good outcome and great work so far. Give him a carrot or an apple for me, probably like that more than my message.

KAREN McDONALD, 52, INGERSOLL,

CANADA"

"Keep hanging in there, I have been thinking of you.

CANDY ALBERT, 57, POTTSTOWN, PA,

UNITED STATES OF AMERICA"

"Happy Friday Barbaro! The rain has stopped here, hopefully there as well so you can spend some time outside & enjoy the beautiful fall weather. You continue to inspire & amaze us all. Stay positive & keep your spirits high.

LOVE & PRAYERS ALWAYS.

ANNAMARIE, 38, PITTSBURGH, PA,

UNITED STATES"

"Stay strong and keep the great attitude. Have a great weekend with lots of treats!

LUCIA, GA"

"Dear Barbaro, Have a good weekend and listen to Dr Richardson. That hoof will be healed before you know it. Kisses and Hugs all weekend.

MICHELE, FT. LAUDERDALE, PA, USA"

"Good morning, Champ: Another acn for the feisty one. Way to go! Your spirit continues to be uplifting for millions. Keep going, champ!

LOVE, DARYL

DARYL SMOLIAK, 58, ST. PAUL, MN, USA"

"Hey Handsome! Thinking of you . . . again!!!! Nothing like the great outdoors . . . enjoy your grazing!! Continue to heal!

LOVE YOU XOXO

SUZY, TAMPA, FL, USA"

"Hi Barbaro—Wishing you a good day and a comfortable weekend. Keep strong and positive—what a shining example you are to us all. God Bless you, M/M Jackson, Dr R & Staff, Michael, and Edgar. I love you, Barbaro.

XOXOXOXO

JEANNE, 48, PEMBROKE PINES, FL, USA"

"FRIDAY . . . BEAUTIFUL DAY AND WONDERFUL NEWS, ABOUT OUR SWEET BARBARO. THANK YOU TO EVERYONE INVOLVED. MAY THE UPCOMING DAYS BE BLESS WITH COMPLETE HEAL-ING AND THE DAY WHEN YOU CAN ROAM IN GREEN PAS-TURES AND SUNSHINE. GOD BLESS ALL OF YOU.

JOAN, 55, BAYTOWN, TX"

"Hey Champ, we are so happy to hear that you are doing so well. You are such a beautiful horse. Thank you to the doctors who are taking such good care of our champ. we love u!

ASHLEY AND SUSAN RUSDEN,
DOWNINGTOWN, PA, USA"

"Way to go Barbaro! What a heart! I cheered for you in the Derby, and I am still cheering for you in life. You are a beautiful animal, and we all here send you all our love and prayers!

SALLY, 56, BROKEN ARROW, OK,
USA"

"Still rooting for you and hope you are better each day.

LOWELL JACKSON, 70, WAYNE, PA,
USA"

"Sweet Barbaro, ACN those have become the three best words for me. Have a good day and say hi to Dr. R and your nice nurses for us.

XOXOXOXOXOXOXO
ROSEMARIE & BRADY,
NEW YORK, NY"

"Morning Bobby J. Have a happy day. I am lighting candles for you and I pray for you and yours everyday! Continue the miracle! God bless you!

JOANNE FRANK, 53, MIDLAND PARK,
NJ"

"Angel Barbaro and Dr. R. Angels. A poem: Angels/Seeing the wonders of God./The heart of love./A pink rose opening/Connecting to all/ You . . . My Sentimental Friends.

LOVE,

DEE, 40, MERRILLVILLE, IN, USA"

"Just to let you know that all of us in the horse community think of you daily and appreciate the work you are doing. You are helping people understand the need for the best services at all of our clinics. Hugs to all and to Barbaro.

BARBARA, 63, ALPHARETTA, GA, USA"

"Hay Barbaro! Friday at Last! You and Dr. Dean, nurses, Mr. and Mrs. Jackson and all your other connections have a great weekend!

LOVE YA, BABY!

LAURA S., 56, SNOHOMISH, WA, USA"

"Good Morning, Gorgeous! Keeping up with you weekly; always looking for more good news; continue to heal for the long run. Thank you NBC for maintaining this site for Barbaro fans and horse lovers everywhere!

RITA WOLFE, OKLAHOMA CITY, OK"

"Barbaro, Keep working to get stronger each day. You have great care there. Someday you will be running in green fields again. My sister thinks you are the greatest horse since Secretariat.

DAN, 55

BEREA, OH, UNITED STATES"

"Hello sweetie pie! We are sending lots of love your way for a wonderful day and comfortable weekend. You are the very best horse and we thank God each and every day for your presence in this world. We pray for you and all animals who suffer.

KARIN, 50, TRENTON, NJ"

"Sweetest Barbaro—I've been thinking about you all week, as always, and I'm glad you are coming along and hope that your weekend will be a good one. Blessings to all those helping you on this journey.

LOVE YOU, BARBARO.
PAM MROSS, 56, FRANKLIN, WI,
USA"

"Morning sweet pea. Think it's gonna be a nice day. Maybe a bit chilly so perhaps you better wear a wrap. I love ya and you happen to be my favorite fella.

LOVE AND KISSES . . . CINDY, 52,
CHEVY CHASE, MD, UNITED STATES"

"Hi Champ! My thoughts and prayers are with you. Enjoy your time outside, stay healthy and just take it a day at a time. Much thanks to Dr. Richardson and his staff—what an awesome job!

JERI"

"Nice to see you are feeling so well. You have come a long way. Take care and God bless.

CLAUDIA, 57,
ANCHORAGE, AK"

"Barbaro, be sure to give your special hug to Dr. Richardson and a sweet nuzzle to Mrs. Jackson. Rest well, enjoy your treats, and know my heart beats for your heart, Barbaro!

LOVE YOU, LOU ANN"

"Beautiful Barbaro! Our Lady, St. Jude & St. Francis watching over you! Positive healing thoughts of sunny meadows to come! My heart beats for your heart, Barbaro! Enjoy your treats!

LOVE YOU & A KISS ON YOUR NOSE!!
LOU ANN, 44, DALLASTOWN, PA, USA"

"Hi Angelface, Your hoof is growing so beautifully and your leg too. I thank the Lord for your healing and your mission. You are a blessing to us all!!! I love you very much.

XXOO, NANCY, SHADOW HILLS, CA,
USA"

"Barbaro, you are such a nut. You can't go the wedding because you have nothing to wear and you can't dance? You send the bride good wishes, but do not yourself plan to be monogamous??? Too much fun.

MARILYN, CA"

"Dear Barbaro, Thinking of you always and always sending you best wishes for a complete recovery. You are an inspiration. Keep up the good work. We love you. Thank you, Bolton Center.

JOY, STOWE, VT, USA"

"Bonjour Barbaro! I have been gone for a while but I have been thinking about you often. Friends would send me photos and news of you so I could keep track of your recovery. I love you so, Barbaro.

LISE, GILEAD, ME, UNITED STATES OF AMERICA"

"My thoughts are with you and your family and friends. As an animal lover, I have been intently waiting for updates. I'm so pleased that you continue to improve and exhibit a strong will to overcome!

MELINDA, 35, MAYSEL, WV, USA"

"Barbaro. I have asked for blessings for you from the Franciscan Sisters of Little Falls MN. Sunday is the Blessing of the Animals. I will be moving so will pray and meditate for you while I move.

MARY, 51, BEMIDJI, MN, USA"

"St. Francis, look lovingly upon Barbaro. Help him heal quickly. Miracles can happen. Help him stay calm and on the mend without incident. Inspire his Doctor to do his best. Amen.

MARY, 51, BEMIDJI, MN, USA"

"Barbaro, have a relaxing weekend. Enjoy the sun and fresh grass. Keep your beautiful spirit shining. You are all that is wonderful in the world. You are a precious Blessing. Keep on fighting. I love you. My Prayers are with you.

ALISSA, 30, WEBSTER, NY, USA"

"Barbaro . . . such a wonderful, dear horse. Happy you continue to make progress . . . and love seeing you enjoy the outdoors! I pray for your continued progress, knowing you are in the best care. Your perseverance is such an inspiration!

JAMIE, 47, LOCKPORT, NY,

USA"

"I was having the worst day, then I checked up on you & your good updates, the love from around the world & your sweet face made my day better. Thanks for being part of my life in a small way & may God Bless you always.

DIANA, GRESHAM, OR, USA"

"I have not heard anything about you for awhile and I'm afraid that I've missed something. Are you O.K. I am a horse lover and have ridden for five years. Be strong! You have captured the heart of many. Including mine.

ERIN, 11, FLOWER MOUND, TX,

UNITED STATES OF AMERICA"

"Dear Barbaro: You will always be in my heart and I wish you a happy, peaceful life. Keep up the good work and recover soon. I love you, Barbaro.

FRANCENE. DAMASCUS,

MONTGOMERY, MD"

"Night night precious boy you will always be my favorite fella. i love ya to pieces.

CINDY, 52, CHEVY CHASE, MD,

UNITED STATES"

"I'm so glad you're doing well, big fella. It's great to hear you get outside when the weather's nice and that you enjoy that. I check up on you every week and you're in my prayers. Keep up the good work and love life, my friend.

MARK, 35, NEWINGTON, CT, USA"

"Wow, buddy! What an inspiration you are! I have been praying for you almost daily since May 20, and you are definitely doing your part. My continued prayer is that you not only 'beat the odds,' but go for the major miracle!

DONNA, 56, PALM DESERT, CA, USA"

"Hi Sweet Boy! I pray for you and check on you every day. You are doing so well!! The entire world has fallen in love with you. Grow, grow, grow hoofies!! We love you B!!

TRACY, 45, BEAVERCREEK, OH, USA"

"My best to a fantastic horse and to all of the vets at the center for their efforts in saving a wonderful animal . . . wishes & prayers that all continues to improve and your efforts are rewarded . . . and Barbaro enjoys many more years as a healthy horse.

CONNIE BELL, 61, SUN CITY, CA,
USA"

"Hi Handsome! You are our favorite horse! You should have been horse of the year. You are a great inspiration to many of us. You are such a fighter! Keep it up big boy! Thx to Dr. Dean.

CHRISSY, HONOLULU, HI, USA"

"Dear Dr. Richardson,

I hope you read this letter. I just wanted to thank you on behalf of all pet owners in America (I own three cats) for the way you help horses with your skill and your kindness. It must be tough on you when you lose one of the horses, but what I admire you about you is that you do it anyway. You are one of the very few but great people in the world who will take in jobs that often end painfully. One thing. If Barbaro doesn't make it—and I believe he will—you have will have nothing to be ashamed of. You are one of the people who, like my father used to say, show up. I wish you well. God bless.

JOAN SEAMAN, DIX HILLS, NY"

"Each day you are in my prayers. You will always be a great champion. Stay strong.

DEBBIE, 51, ST. LOUIS, MO, USA"

"Hello, Cutie This weekend I'll be going away for several days. I will have access to a computer and so will check in daily. Normally I check in several times a day! Good Grazing. I'll keep those prayers coming.

NATALIE, STAMFORD, CT, USA"

"We're thrilled that you are doing better. Keep your spirit up and you will do fine.

LIS LUCAS, 58, LUTHERVILLE, MD, USA"

"Hi buddy! PLEASE GET BETTER SOON! I love you!

EM, 12, RICHMOND, RI, USA"

"Barbaro, I still pray for you and I am very pleased at your progress. You are a winner and soon you will be completely healed. I LOVE YOU!!! A special THANKS to the Drs who care for you daily. GOD BLESS EACH OF YOU!!!!

> KAREN, INDIANAPOLIS, IN, USA"

"Dear Barbaro, After 4 months, your many devoted fans still think of you each day. We wish all the best to you and your staff. Grow, hoof, grow!

> YOUR PAL, XENA
> RENNE, DURHAM, NC, USA"

"Dear Barbaro: We wish you good health and many happy years in a beautiful pasture making little Barbaros.

> LIZ AND DAVE, MILWAUKEE, WI, USA"

"Dear Barbaro,

It's been around six months since your triumphant win of the 132nd Kentucky Derby, four months since your horrific accident at Pimlico, which brought tears to my eyes then as well as every time I've heard or have read anything about it since. You are a horse of great courage, one that has touched the nation like no other in history. I was watching you as you crossed the finish line of the Kentucky Derby, my mom and dad took me to see the race. You were fantastic. I will always remember that day and how fast and strong you were. I also watched you at the Preakness, but from TV this time. We watched from early in the morning, getting to relive your glory day at the Derby and the anticipation of waiting for you to race again was great. When the accident occurred I cried for you, as did my mom and dad, but not my little brother because he didn't really understand what was happening. For days afterward we watched you on the news and prayed for your full recovery every night. I want you to know I haven't forgotten about you and I don't think I ever will. You will always be in my heart.

Apples & Carrots—for you that's hugs and kisses.

S. B. NORTHEAST, PENNSYLVANIA"

Don't think that Barbaro's not grateful for all the love he's experienced. In early November 2006, an award dinner of the National Turf Writers Association presented an award to "Team Barbaro"— the group consisted of Barbaro himself, owners Roy and Gretchen Jackson, trainer Michael Matz, assistant trainer and exercise rider Peter Brette, and jockey Edgar Prado—it was the "Mr. Fitz Award." This is given to a person or group typifying the spirit of racing; the award is named for the late Racing Hall of Fame trainer Jim "Sunny Jim" Fitzsimmons.

"The injury to Barbaro this spring was adversity of the most wrenching kind," said the presenter, Bill Nack. "Team Barbaro acquitted themselves so well [in the midst of the catastrophe] that I suspect they ended up with more admirers and friends around the world than they would have if Barbaro had won the Triple Crown."

After they received the award, Roy Jackson said that Barbaro had asked him to make some remarks on his behalf. "He wants to first honor you men and women of the press for your honest and straightforward reporting of this whole event. You've done a great service to the racing industry." Jackson cited the subjects of laminitis and the antislaughter bill. "Barbaro also wants to thank the multitude of people who sent notes, carrots, you name it," he continued. "Lastly, he wanted to thank Dean Richardson and the whole staff at New Bolton for the care they've given him."

Jackson related Barbaro's "requests" for Richardson to display his dancing talents during morning medical rounds, and finally, for the veterinarian to speed up his treatments because he's ready to "bring on the girls."

Glossary of Horse-racing Terms

AGENT: A person authorized to act, for a fee, on the behalf of a jockey or racehorse owner. Generally refers to a jockey's agent, who lines up rides for him or her.

ALLOWANCE RACES: Refers to allowing weight to be taken off, based on the horses in the race not having won certain other races. An allowance horse race may have wins in lower-level races but no wins in higher-level races such as stakes races, maiden, and claiming.

APPRENTICE: A rider who has not ridden a specified number of winning racehorses within a certain time period. These riders get weight allowances on all their mounts, based on the number of winners they have. Ten pounds until the fifth winner, 7 pounds until the 35th winner, and 5 pounds for one calendar year after the date of the 5th winner.

BACKING: A thoroughbred first learns to accept a rider's weight in a procedure known as "backing," usually done in its stall. Backing involves a person standing beside and facing the horse, gradually shifting his weight onto the horse's back.

BACKSTRETCH: The area where horses are cared for and prepared for competition (most such areas are located behind the track's backstretch). Here a groom looks after a thoroughbred's creature comforts: the farrier measures and fits lightweight racing shoes or plates on the horse. Grooms wrap bandages around the horse's fragile legs; exercise riders gallop their charges during a morning workout; grooms "cool out" horses after a workout. The presence of cats, roosters, goats, or other stable mascots seems to have a calming effect on temperamental horses.

BAY: A horse's color, which varies greatly. It may be yellowish tan to brown, or a rich dark shade of mahogany sometimes called a dark bay (like Barbaro) with black "points"—black mane, tail, and shading or black found low on the legs.

BLAZE: A white patch on the horse's forehead (Barbaro could be easily identified by his blaze, which was shaped like a diamond. His dam, La Ville Rouge, also had a blaze on her forehead).

BLINKERS: Solid cuplike devices worn over a horse's eyes to focus his vision in the direction that a trainer thinks will do him the most good. For example, the 1941 Triple Crown winner Whirlaway sometimes ran diagonally across the track and completed the race using the outside rail as a guide. Trainer Ben A. Jones fitted him with one blinker on the side of his right eye so he couldn't see the rail but followed the inside rail, where there was no blinker in the way.

BREAK DOWN: When a horse is injured in a race and can't continue. Once a trainer cost "Black Gold"—the 1924 Derby winner who captured the hearts of Americans as the "people's horse"—his life. He was trained by an obese alcoholic named Hanley Webb, who treated him badly while training, then returned him to racing when he was in poor condition, prompting his regular jockey to refuse to ride him. And in the end, running lame in a race, he broke a leg and had to be put down. Webb denied that he knew the horse was lame, but this simply wasn't true. That was sad and shocking, but for pure shock it would be hard to beat what was to occur three months after the 1975 Kentucky Derby. A match race was arranged at Belmont Park between "Foolish Pleasure" and the Derby winner, "Ruffian," a speedy black filly, Horse of the Year, and a fan favorite. Millions tuned in to watch it on TV.

At first, Foolish Pleasure led, but by the time they got into the backstretch, Ruffian had gained the lead. The two horses were flying, and then, just like that, Ruffian snapped her right hind leg, ran on for a few strides, and stopped. There was nothing anyone could do. She was put down and buried in the infield of Belmont Park. People who saw it happen will likely never forget it.

BRED: Horses cohabiting to produce a foal. (*See* "Covering.")

BREEDING: Refers to the process of mixing and matching of racehorses in breeding to produce championship runners. Horse breeding started in England when three Englishmen imported three Arabian stallions from the Mediterranean and started to breed them with the strong English horse. The two pedigrees blended beautifully, the English horse contributing strength and endurance, and Arabian horses, speed. Races were conducted in England with thoroughbreds, and then some of these horses were transported to America, where breeding continued further. Originally, men bred horses just for sport and for competition, but the Civil War was to change that. Many southern gentlemen had been financially wiped out by the war, and they had to find a way to make a living. Since the terrain they lived in—particularly Kentucky—had the kind of country and grass that was ideal for training thoroughbreds, breeding stables started to spring up and men bred, sold, and raced horses. From that day until this, money has been in the equation.

BREEZING: A horse running at moderate speed. Refers to the concept of "breezing along."

BUGLER: The bugler sounds the familiar "first call" as the horses step onto the track before each race.

CAMERAS: Film-patrol cameras record every step of the race as well as capturing the order of the finish.

CLAIMING RACES: Here, horses race with a price tag on their heads. The owner wants to sell them with the least trouble, so he enters them in a race and they're for sale at a certain price. Before the races start, men who want to buy horses put up the monies specified on the price tag. When the race is over, the person who put up the money owns the horse no matter how poorly he performed, or even if he died. And if the horse won the race, too bad: The old owner gets the purse money. Claiming races come in a wide range of classes based on the price of the horses for sale. The highest level is the optional claimer, usually at a high price like $75,000 or more, where the horses can be entered for claiming or not at the owner's discretion. Regular claiming races can go from $1,000 to $100,000, with the high end found only at major tracks like Belmont or Santa Anita, and with the low end only at minor tracks like Portland Meadows or Great Lakes Downs.

CONNECTIONS: These are the important people surrounding a racehorse, like the owners, trainer, exercise rider, and so on.

COVERING: The physical act of a mare and sire mating. To begin, the mare is "teased" by a "teaser stallion" to make sure she is in heat, and this is indicated, among other ways, by her vulva opening and closing, her raising her tail and showing interest in the stallion. As a final precaution, to make sure she is in heat, a vet palpates her ovaries. Once she is in the breeding shed, the people there will "tease" her again, and then breeding will occur. The mare is normally pregnant for 11 months.

CRASH KIT: A kit containing all syringes, needles, and medications needed to stabilize or revive a mare or foal who is born with a life-threatening problem. Bill Sanborn says that he needed a crash kit only three times in his life; once, when he didn't have it, the foal died, and the other two times he believed his use of the crash kit saved the foal.

DAM: The female parent of a foal.

FILLY: A young female horse. In horse racing, fillies normally carry five pounds less then do colts.

FOAL: A baby horse. Most thoroughbreds in the Northern Hemisphere are born in the spring. (Regardless of the actual date, January 1 is the official "birthday" of all foals.) The youngster will spend its formative months playing with other colts and fillies and growing in size and ability.

FOALED: When a baby horse is born.

FOALING: The process of a mare giving birth to a baby horse.

FOUNDATION SIRES: The three thoroughbreds imported to England from the East, out of whom were bred all thoroughbreds. They are: (1) The Byerly Turk (1680–1696), captured from the Turks in Hungary. He was brought to England by Colonel Robert Byerley. Due to a printer's error, the horse's name was registered in the General Stud Book without the final "e." (2) The Godolphin Arabian (1724–1753). Given by the bey of Tunis to the king of France, he was purchased by Edward Coke and subsequently presented to the earl of Godolphin, who studded him. He sired the champion mare "Aelima," imported to Maryland in 1750. (3) The Darley Arabian (1700–1733). Thomas Darley sent this Arabian stallion from Syria to England. Ninety percent of all thoroughbreds today are descended through his son, "Flying Childers," and his great-great grandson, "Eclipse."

GELDING: A horse whose testicles have been surgically removed. The most common reason for this is to calm down a horse's personality. But it doesn't mean that he will lose his speed and stamina, as it does with other creatures. There have been many championship horses who were geldings, the latest being Funny Cide, winner of the 2005 Kentucky Derby.

GRADE 1 RACES: The most important grade of all races, featuring the top horses.

GROOM: The person who takes care of one or more horses, washing, grooming, and feeding them. Good grooms are important because their hands-on care of the horse sends a message, fair or foul. Grooms usually get to be very close to the horses, maybe closer than anyone else. For example, "Sir Barton," a dark, muscular colt who won the 1919 Triple Crown, was characterized by J. K. Ross, son of his owner, as an "irascible, exasperating creature . . . downright evil. He had no interest in other horses and he completely ignored and despised all human beings. With the possible exception of his groom, a huge and dark-skinned man by the name of Toots Thompson who worshipped his charge."

HAND: The unit, a human hand, used to measure a horse. A hand equals 4" or so, and a horse is measured from his withers down. So a horse that is 16 hands high would measure 64" (4" × 16") from the ground and would be considered about average. A horse that is 17 hands is quite a bit larger.

HAND-RIDDEN: A manner of riding in which a jockey rides a horse without striking him on a flank with a whip. Edgar Prado "hand-rode" Barbaro to victory in the Kentucky Derby. Some jockeys hand-ride their horses because they have no choice—they have dropped their whips.

HOT WALKER: A person who walks a horse after it works out to cool it down.

JOCKEY CLUB: The Jockey Club, established in 1894, is the governing body for all thoroughbred racing in America. It keeps the pedigrees and race records of all horses as well. It functions like the American Kennel Club does for dogs.

JOCKEY RIDING TECHNIQUE: Jockeys sat upright until the end of the last century, when a man named Tod Sloan developed the exaggerated forward-seat position. Placing the rider's weight over the horse's center of gravity greatly reduces wind resistance and, more important, keeps a rider in greater balance with a horse at high speeds.

JOCKEY WEIGHT: To ensure that each horse will carry the precise assigned weight, jockeys and their equipment weigh "out" before, and weigh "in" after, a race. Weight is an ever-present factor in a jockey's life. Few weigh more than 115 pounds, and those who have difficulty with excess poundage must diet constantly.

There is no question that some jockeys are bulimic, which can lead to loss of strength and other problems. Many years ago, the practice of eating, then vomiting, was known as "flipping." It was this practice that killed a number of great early jockeys, including Isaac Murphy, who was thought by many experts to be the greatest jockey who ever lived. (While many great jockeys compile a winning percentage of 20 percent, Isaac Murphy's was 44 percent.)

LAMINITIS: A disease that horses can develop in their hooves that destroys the laminae, or the connective tissue between the bottom coffin bone in the foot. Despite huge advances in modern medicine, doctors have yet to find a surefire way to prevent it. It is usually related to how much weight a horse puts on its hoofs.

LOOK OF EAGLES: Old-time horse breeders feel that horses who have great potential have a certain look in their eye, a "look of eagles." Knowing. Confident. Fierce. As mentioned earlier, the 1992 Kentucky Derby winner Lil E. Tee was selected by an owner because he had that look in his eyes. Another bidder saw the same look, but his bid was a piddling $1,000 less than that of the man who won the horse.

LUG IN (OR OUT): When a horse gets tired, he starts to drift left or right, and it's the job of the jockey to keep him on a straight course. Many a jockey has ridden a horse in the last part of its stretch who lugs in or out. Then the jockey must use all his skills to enable the horse to get to the wire first.

MAIDEN RACE: Refers to the first time a horse wins a race. The horse "breaks" his or her maiden. Horses that are considered superior to other horses run in a "maiden special weight" race. There are also maiden-claiming races for the horses who failed in maiden-special-weight company or who are not thought to be good enough to start out higher.

MARE: A female horse who is more than five years old. (Horses, by the way, can live into their 20s and sometimes 30s, but sometimes for a much shorter time. For example, Canonero II, the winner of the 1971 Derby, lived only to 13, and Swale, the Kentucky Derby winner, died as a three-year-old. One day, outside his barn, he just keeled over and died. Most people thought he had had a heart attack. Bizarre, but true.

MORNING WORKOUTS: Whether on a farm or at a track, thoroughbreds are galloped in morning workouts to keep them in racing trim.

OUTRIDERS: Outriders escort the horses to the post in a race, then wait to catch any that might throw their jockeys and bolt. Outriders also assist in case there is trouble in a race, such as in false starts. When Barbaro broke from the gate early in the 2006 Derby, the outriders were there to get him under control.

PEDIGREE: The word used to describe the familial background that produced a particular horse. The more champions in the pedigree of a particular horse, the more potential value it has. One young horse went for $13 million. And "Fusaichi Pegasus" went for almost $5 million.

PONYING: Leading the horse around a training track to develop wind and muscle.

RACING GEAR: Weighing no more than four pounds, a racing saddle is little more than a "postage stamp-sized" leather pad. The whip is also called a "bat." Goggles protect against mud and dirt. Some jockeys wear multiple pairs, so, as they ride, if one pair gets covered with dirt, they can flip it down so they can see through the remaining pairs. The difference between assigned weight and the rider's actual poundage is made up by lead bars carried in saddle cloth pockets (some types of races require better horses to carry more weight as a handicap).

SILKS: Like coats of arms, the distinctive colors and designs on shirts and caps identify horse and rider. Every owner registers his "silks" with the Jockey Club, the sport's registry and ruling body. Inside the jockey's room is a beehive of activities between races, as riders shower and switch silks while valets take care of equipment.

SIRE: The male horse who impregnates the female and fathers the foal. As mentioned in "Covering," the mare usually goes to the sire's "breeding shack" to be bred.

STAKES RACES: Races in which the top horses race. They have the highest "purses," although the amount can vary widely from a small track to a major one, and carry the most prestige when winning. Stakes races run from small local stakes for a few thousand dollars to the Breeders' Cup Classic for $5 million. Obviously, the class difference between the two extremes is quite wide.

Local stakes are where you will find the best local horses, while graded stakes will have top horses both from the local trainers and from other locations. Local stakes will often have restrictions such as the horse having to be bred in the particular state or to have raced at the local track. These are called restricted stakes.

The top level for stakes races is the "graded-stakes" races, and these have no restrictions other than age or sex. There are three grades, and the grade assigned a race is controlled by the "Graded Stakes Committee," which ensures that a grade 1, 2, or 3 race is the same class level, regardless of what track it is being run at. The grades are reviewed each year based on the performances of the horses coming from those races and are adjusted up or down as needed. Most mid-size or larger tracks will have at least one grade 3 race, while large tracks like Belmont Park or Churchill Downs will have several of all grades.

There were 734 unrestricted U.S. stakes races in 2005 with a purse of at least $75,000, and 475 of those were assigned graded status for 2006 after being reviewed. 104 were assigned grade 1, 160 to grade 2, and 211 to grade 3. Grade 1 races include the Kentucky Derby, Preakness, Belmont Stakes, and all eight Breeders' Cup races. Horses running in these are the cream of the crop, and a horse who is competitive here but can't win should always be watched when dropping to a lower grade of race.

STALLION: A male horse.

STARTER: After his assistants load the horses into their stalls, the starter waits until all are standing quietly before pressing the button to open the gate.

STARTING GATE TRAINING: A horse must be introduced to the race starting gate and learn to leave quickly and cleanly. The gate locks the horse in mechanically from behind and in front, but the front gate is easy to open because it is held closed magnetically by an electric charge.

STEWARDS: People who enforce racing rules and assess penalties for any infractions committed in a race.

TACK: A jockey's horseback-riding equipment.

THOROUGHBRED: A racehorse developed from the Foundation Sires. It has a refined head with widely spaced, intelligent eyes and a neck that is somewhat longer and lighter than in other breeds. The withers are high and well defined, leading to an evenly curved back. The shoulder is deep, well-muscled, and extremely sloped, while the "heart girth" is deep and relatively narrow. The legs are clean and long with pronounced tendons, and move smoothly in unison through one plane. The bone structure of the upper hind leg makes room for long, strong muscling. The thighbone is long, and the angle it makes with the hipbone is wide. The powerful muscling of the hip and thigh continues to the "gaskin," which is set low. Coat colors in thoroughbreds may be bay, dark bay, chestnut, black, or gray; roans are seen only rarely. White markings are frequently seen on both the face and legs.

TIMERS: Photoelectric timers show how fast the front runner is going and give the winner's time in fifths of a second.

TRAINER: The individual responsible for getting a horse ready to race. A thoroughbred's development, exercise, and daily care are planned and supervised by its trainer, who also decides when a horse should race and who will be its jockey.

TRAINING: This includes galloping around a track, getting "broken" to the saddle, and learning how to leave a starting gate.

WEANED: The point at which a foal stops feeding off its mother, usually at the age of five months.

YEARLING: Having spent its first year developing size and power, the young thoroughbred begins training as a yearling. The animal learns to accept a saddle and bridle, allow a rider on its back, and ultimately to break from a starting gate and gallop around a track—all the skills necessary to be a racehorse

YEARLING SALES: Some yearlings (year-old horses) are kept by their breeders or sold privately. Others are auctioned at such places as the Keeneland Sales in Lexington, Kentucky. Prospective purchasers examine the horses, study their pedigrees, then bid. The record price paid for a thoroughbred yearling was more than $13 million.

Help Us to Stop Horse Slaughter in the United States!

*E*very year, almost 100,000 horses, many of them race horses, some only babies, are slaughtered in the United States, and the meat shipped over seas for consumption in countries whose laws allow it. Barbaro escaped that fate because he had loving owners with the will and wherewithal to save him and, failing that, making sure that he would die in dignity and peace.

But many horses do not have such caring people in their lives, and they need help—from us and you. The only way to stop this inhumane practice is for us all to get involved: learn via the Internet where and how, horse slaughter occurs, and then explore the groups that are arrayed against it, and do whatever your time and motivation allows. (One good place to start is The Humane Society of The United States.)

Before going to these sites, however, be aware that some of the details you will encounter are X-rated for cruelty and violence. It is not for the fainthearted.

One hopeful note is that Congress is well aware of the practice and legislation prohibiting it was almost passed and should come up again soon for consideration. We should all be there when it does. Each and every one of us can make a difference.

In the book, someone gave us the best reason of all for trying to save Barbaro, and it is still the best reason for trying to save horses headed to the slaughterhouse: "Not killing a mockingbird is what makes us human."

We hope you will join us and the many others that are making it their personal mission to do whatever they can to put a stop to this horrific practice. These animals need our voice and our help.

In love—and hope,
TOM AND PAM

GET THE FACTS ON
HORSE SLAUGHTER

How many horses are slaughtered each year?
Each year nearly 100,000 horses are slaughtered in the United States and processed for human consumption. In addition, many thousands of live horses are transported across the border to Canada for slaughter. After these horses are killed, their flesh is shipped to Europe and Asia for human consumption. Their owners are often totally unaware of the pain, fear, and suffering their horses endure before being slaughtered.

Who eats horse meat?
Horse meat is not eaten in the United States; it is exported to serve specialty markets overseas. The largest markets are France, Belgium, Holland, Japan, and Italy. The only three horse slaughter plants in the United States are foreign owned.

How do unwanted, surplus horses end up at slaughterhouses?
Most horses destined for slaughter are sold at livestock auctions or sales. The cruelty of horse slaughter is not limited to the act of killing the animals. Horses bound for slaughter are shipped, frequently for long distances, in a manner that fails to accommodate their unique temperaments. They are usually not rested, fed, or watered during travel. Economics, not humane considerations, dictate the conditions, including crowding as many horses into trucks as possible.

Often, terrified horses and ponies are crammed together and transported to slaughter in double-deck trucks designed for cattle and pigs. The truck ceilings are so low that the horses are not able to hold their heads in a normal, balanced position. Inappropriate floor surfaces lead to slips and falls, and sometimes even trampling. Some horses arrive at the slaughterhouse seriously injured or dead. Although transportation accidents have largely escaped public scrutiny, several tragic incidents involving collapsed upper floors and overturned double-deckers have caused human fatalities, as well as suffering and death for the horses.

How are the horses killed?

Under federal law, horses are required to be rendered unconscious prior to slaughter, usually with a device called a captive bolt gun, which shoots a metal rod into the horse's brain. Some horses, however, are improperly stunned and are conscious when they are hoisted by a rear leg to have their throats cut. In addition, conditions in the slaughterhouse are stressful and frightening for horses.

Which kinds of horses are affected?

Horses of virtually all ages and breeds are slaughtered, from draft types to miniatures. Horses commonly slaughtered include unsuccessful race horses, horses who are lame or ill, surplus riding school and camp horses, mares whose foals are not economically valuable, and foals who are "by-products" of the Pregnant Mare Urine (PMU) industry, which produces the estrogen-replacement drug Premarin®. Ponies, mules, and donkeys are slaughtered as well. Many of the horses that HSUS investigators have seen purchased for slaughter were in good health, and bought for only a few hundred dollars.

Are there any federal or state laws protecting horses from these cruelties?

A few states (California, Connecticut, New York, Pennsylvania, Vermont, and Virginia) have laws that are intended to prevent some of these abuses. Unfortunately, even in these states, enforcement is inadequate, as evidenced by the continuing use of double-deck trucks even where they are illegal.

Congress passed the Commercial Transportation of Equines for Slaughter Act in March 1996, which directed the U.S. Department of Agriculture (USDA) to write regulations to enforce the Act. Those regulations were not released until January 2002. Unfortunately, the regulations allow the use of double-deck trailers for an additional five years; permit horses to be transported for 28 hours without food, water, or rest; and allow the transport companies themselves to certify the care the horses received.

What is The Humane Society of the United States (HSUS) doing to protect horses?

We are working with bipartisan leaders in Congress to end this terrible and utterly unnecessary practice. Recent passage of the Sweeney-Spratt Agriculture Appropriations amendment to prevent tax supported horse slaughter demonstrated the strong political will to ban horse slaughter. The amendment passed in a landslide 269–158 vote—carrying leaders from parties and members of the agriculture committee. Until horses are no longer slaughtered for food, which is the ultimate goal of The HSUS, we believe that their suffering must be lessened to the greatest extent possible. The HSUS will continue to participate in the process by which the USDA develops and enforces regulations to police this industry. In addition, The HSUS will continue to assist states in the passage of effective laws that will govern the treatment of horses sold for slaughter within their borders.

What alternatives exist to slaughtering horses for human consumption?

Several alternatives exist, such as humane euthanasia performed by a veterinarian. The bodies of euthanized horses can be picked up by rendering plants for disposal. Horse owners can have their animals euthanized and bury them (where permissible) or have them cremated. Another option is to donate the horse to an equine rescue organization; some will take unwanted horses and find them good homes. The horse racing industry recently initiated the Ferdinand

Fee which will be used to fund retirement homes for race horses to ensure that no more racehorses like Ferdinand wind up at a slaughterhouse.

What can individuals do to lessen the suffering of horses bound for slaughter?

Individuals can support organizations such as The HSUS that work toward the goal of ending horse slaughter. One of our goals is to reduce the callous overbreeding of both sport horses and pleasure horses so that older, injured, or surplus animals will no longer be viewed as expendable. A reduced number of surplus horses would result in a sharp decline in the profits of the horse meat industry because the cost of obtaining each horse would rise due to decreased availability. This would force slaughterhouses to scale down their operations and eventually shut down. Horse owners should think carefully before breeding a mare and consider adopting their next horse from an equine rescue organization.

Horse owners can plan for their animal's eventual death by setting aside funds for humane euthanasia by a veterinarian, if it becomes necessary. Menopausal women on hormone replacement therapy can ask their doctors to prescribe one of the many safe and effective, FDA-approved alternatives to Premarin®. (Contact The HSUS for a free brochure detailing these alternatives.) Finally, individuals can work within their home states to pass laws that afford stronger protections for slaughter-bound horses.

Photo and Illustration Credits

BARBARO

APRIL 29, 2003 TO JANUARY 29, 2007

Love makes the world go round.
—**Saint Thomas Aquinas.**

*I*n the early 20th century there was a doctor who worked for the New York City Health Department named Sara Josephine Baker. She was an expert on children's health, particularly babies who lived in the slums of the Lower East Side of New York, and one day, a New York foundling hospital where orphan babies in the city were kept called her, desperate. Something strange and scary was happening. Every other orphan baby who was admitted—half of them—were dying, despite an ultrasanitary environment, germ-free milk (contaminated milk was a problem at the time), nutritious and plentiful food, and the best of medical care.

Baker investigated and found the babies small, frail, and sickly. But there were two babies who seemed to be thriving. They were pink, fat, and sassy—stars of the ward.

Why?

Baker pondered the problem, including discussing it at the

office with colleagues. Neither she nor they could figure it out. And 50 percent of the babies continued to die.

Then, like a homicide detective, she went to the orphanage's administration with a question. Were the two babies that were thriving treated any differently from the others?

The answer was no, but then Baker expanded her investigation, staying for hours, watching how the babies were cared for and for anything unusual. She noticed that the care given the babies by the nurses was "cold": Babies were picked up to be fed, or washed, etc.—but that was it.

Then one day, she decided to observe the babies at night. And that was when that she noticed that one of cleaning ladies went to the two fat and sassy babies, and one by one, picked them up, hugged them, cooed to them . . . nurtured them. Baker questioned her and learned that she did this every night that she worked, but only with those particular babies. They were her favorites.

Baker got it: The babies who were treated with care thrived; those who weren't treated that way were at serious risk of dying.

Baker presented her conclusion to the orphanage's administration. She said that she wanted to ship the sickly babies to immigrant mothers and let them take care of them. The tenements they lived in may have been ugly, but the mothering was beautiful. Within two years, the rate of orphan deaths had dropped by 50 percent. It continued to go down as the years went by. What made the difference was a single thing: nurturing . . . also known as love.

Time after time after time, it has been shown that all creatures— human or otherwise—do better when they are loved, cared for.

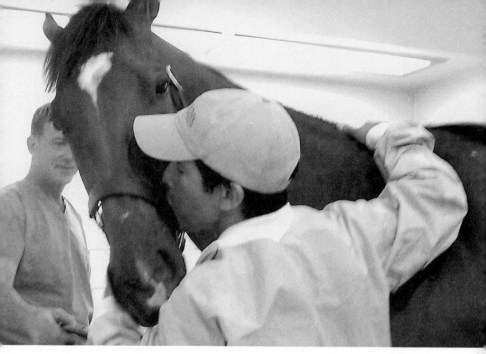

If only love could heal

There are various theories about why this occurs, including the theory that love releases certain potent disease-fighting agents from the brain, but no one seems certain of what happens, just that love works.

TIME TO SAY GOODBYE

In late January of 2007 Barbaro's health worsened. He developed laminitis in his two front feet and a deep abscess in his right hind leg. Worse still, the actual pain he was feeling was judged to be more than he could tolerate comfortably. The Jacksons and his medical team had always stated that he would not suffer, and the ultimate decision was made. At 10:30 AM on Monday, January 29, 2007, Barbaro received a slight overdose of anesthetic and he was euthanized. "It could not have been more peaceful," Dr. Richardson said.

But he did not die in vain. In fact there are many positive and wonderful things the world has gained from Barbaro's fight.

Once again we were reminded, as Dr. Baker had learned many years ago, about the power of love. No question that Barbaro fought harder because somewhere inside that great heart he knew that people loved him, that he mattered. He put up a great struggle to match the love of his owners, and doctors and other caregivers, and the millions of ordinary people from all over the world.

And we learned from his struggle that there are other horses who need our help, that not everybody has the wherewithal and means of his owners. So the Barbaro Fund was established to help other horses and, as of these writing, more than 1.2 million dollars has been contributed.

We also learned about the terrible world of horse slaughter, and the horrific end that many horses come to. Thanks to the coverage of Barbaro there are now many more people involved in helping to fight this ghoulish practice.

In what may prove to be the most significant lesson, the Veterinary medical community learned a great deal about how to handle and treat such injuries as Barbaro's. Indeed, Dr. Richardson, one of the greatest equine surgeons in the world, said: "If I had a horse come in with the same injury tomorrow, I honestly believe I'd have a better chance of saving his life and that's probably because I wouldn't make the same mistakes."

And we learned, again, what defines us as human beings: the love and caring we can give to other creatures. We cannot, as we've said before, let that hummingbird die. It's what makes us human. So, so many people proved that adage with this great horse.

It is, of course, sad that Barbaro is gone. But we know, too, that we will never forget him. Maybe with a tear, but joy too. We will never forget his electrifying run—"It's all Barbaro!"—to the wire in the Kentucky Derby, and his beautiful personality and the heroic fight he waged for his brief life. In a way, he's still running and he will be running for a long, long time.

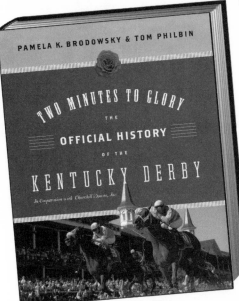